Leisure Crafts

Leisure Crafts

HAMLYN
London · New York · Sydney · Toronto

Published in association with Search Press Limited
by The Hamlyn Publishing Group Limited
London · New York · Sydney · Toronto
Astronaut House, Feltham, Middlesex, England

© Copyright Search Press Limited and
The Hamlyn Publishing Group Limited 1973
Second Impression 1975

ISBN 0 600 35481 4

Printed in Spain by Mateu Cromo, Madrid

Contents

Candle Making

Candles first evolved thousands of years ago as a light source. As time has passed, they have been made of different materials depending on availability; before the discovery of paraffin wax in 1854, tallow and beeswax were mainly used, but several other mixtures have also been found suitable for candlemaking, including rare bayberry wax, spermazetti wax, stearic acid, beeswax and tallow. However, the most economical and commonly used mixture today is paraffin wax and stearin or stearic acid, and this we will call candlewax. When we refer to paraffin wax in this Chapter we mean plain wax *without* stearic acid.

You will find wax a most interesting material to work with. You can mould it with your hands, pour it into all kinds of moulds and casts, and even sculpture your own shapes. Try making your own moulds out of all kinds of materials—not just buying ready-made ones. Experiments with different colours are fun too. Each candle that you make by hand will be more or less unique and you will find that you can make them in all colours and shapes at a fraction of what they cost to buy. This book will help you with some ideas and the basic techniques but you will soon find that you will want to try your own experiments.

The candles that you make are not only useful, but should be used as decorations in the home and lit on suitable occasions.

Do not try too difficult candles at first. Like all things it takes time to acquire the necessary skills and techniques. Don't be disheartened by failures either. Remember you can always melt down a 'dud' candle and re-use the wax. But don't forget that if you melt down a multi-coloured candle, the resulting colour of the wax will be a blend of all your original colours.

BASIC MATERIALS

Before attempting any candles you must first of all assemble the following materials. Some of these you will already have, but most of them you will have to get from a local supplier.

Materials

Paraffin wax
Stearin
Wax dyes
Wicks (in various sizes)
Thermometer (kitchen thermometer, not a room or body one as this will break)
Various pans and/or double boiler
Oil soluble perfumes (only if you wish to give your candles a perfume)
Beeswax sheets (if you are making beeswax candles)
Mould seal (or plasticine or clay)

The most frequently used paraffin wax is one with a melting temperature of 56°–58°C (133°–136°F), although waxes of higher and lower melting temperatures can also be employed for different effects. Paraffin wax ranges from white to cream in colour and can be bought either in block or powder form. Always check the maker's instructions. If you buy a block, a sharp blow with a hammer will break it into reasonable sized pieces.

Wax dyes are the best colouring agent for paraffin wax. They come in either powder or solid form, and should be used according to the maker's instructions. Powdered dyes are usually very concentrated, so care has to be taken not to put in too much. In most cases a small 'pinch' will adequately colour 1 pint of liquid wax. (Don't forget that generally dyes stain everything, including hands!) If a candle is dyed too darkly, it will lessen the glowing effect, because the greater the amount of dye, the less light will be diffused. Solid dyes are less economical,

but they allow a greater degree of accuracy.

Stearin is a white, flaky non-corrosive and non-toxic material. Most dyes should be dissolved in a small amount of heated stearin before being added to the paraffin wax, to ensure full suspension of colour. Usually, the proportion is 10% stearin to wax, (or 1lb stearin to 10lb paraffin wax). This percentage of stearin will also help to release the candle from its mould by causing the wax mixture to shrink a little and thus slip out easily. Stearin also makes the candle opaque.

The 10% stearin must be melted in a separate saucepan and the dye sprinkled or scraped onto it. This mixture should be heated and stirred gently until all the dye is disolved into a coloured liquid and there are no dye particles left on the base of the pan. Then it is added to molten paraffin wax. Heat the candle wax to pouring temperature about 82°C (180°F), and transfer it to a warmed jug for easier pouring. A double boiler is ideal for melting paraffin wax, but you can make do with an ordinary saucepan, providing the heat is not too great. In any case, wax should never be heated over a fierce flame.

Use a thermometer that has a range of up to 204°C (400°F). Never leave a thermometer in setting wax, and don't try to pick set wax off a thermometer to clean it, because it will break if you do. Clean it by dipping in hot water.

Oil soluble perfume (*not* spirit based) can be added at the last possible moment in the making process. Perfumes are best used sparingly to give a delicate aroma rather than a full-bodied smell.

Candles are made to be burned, so wicks are very important. The size of the wick chosen must take into consideration the height and breadth of the candle. If the wick is the right size for the candle, an even, non-smoky flame and a smooth-melting candle will result. As a general rule, the bigger the candle, the larger the wick. If the wick is too small, an excess of molten wax will probably flood the candle. If the wick is too large, there will be insufficient fuel and the wick will burn itself into a smoky flame. If you want a candle to burn and leave behind a hollow shell of wax, use a slightly smaller wick than usual.

Six points to remember are:

1. Ensure that the wick is central.
2. Trim the wick to 8mm ($\frac{1}{4}$in) before lighting.
3. Keep burning candles out of a draught.
4. Keep the burning area of the wax clean (shreds of wick and old match sticks will clog the wick).
5. Give your candle time to burn properly. About 30 minutes burning should establish whether all is well or not.
6. Extinguish your candle properly by push-

ing the wick into the pool of wax. This stops smouldering and ensures a well-waxed wick when the candle is re-lit.

It is possible to make your own wicks by soaking stranded-cotton (previously bleached) in boracic acid, but it is advisable to buy them ready made. Suppliers will give instructions as to which size wick to use.

WARNING!

Hot wax will ignite and react in exactly the same way as boiling fat. Treat hot wax with great care. *Never* put it over a fierce flame. Use a double boiler if possible. *Never* fill any pot too full. Asbestos mats will help when using gas or open flames.

DIPPING—THE OLDEST METHOD OF CANDLEMAKING

The great advantage of dipping is that it involves little pouring. All you need is a pot or jug a little taller than the length of the required candle. Fill the pot with undyed wax and heat it. Tie a length of wick to a stick and dip this into the paraffin wax, heated to 82°C (180°F). Then remove it. Repeat this process at 30 second intervals, this being the time it will take for each coat of wax to harden, until the candle is as thick as you want it. Hang the finished candles to cool (see illustration, top right). If you want the candles to be white and straight, simply let them harden, cutting the wick from the stick and trimming neatly.

If you want a more exciting finish, you can dip the white candles in colour. An economical way of doing this is to float a layer of about 5cm (2in) of coloured molten candle wax on water that has been heated to 82°C (180°F). When using this method, remember to leave some space at the top of the container, because the candle to be dipped will displace some of the water. Remember, too, that it is possible for the water to be at a temperature of, say 93°C (200°F), even though the wax has still not reached 82°C (180°F). If a scum forms it can easily be spooned off.

The white candle is dipped through the candle wax into the water, and then pulled out, thus picking up colour on the way in and on the way out. If the wax is too hot, hardly any colour will be picked up. If the wax is too cool, the candle will be scaly and flaky. This dipping process is continued until the required depth of colour is reached.

If the candle is to be straight and coloured throughout, it is advisable to give a final dip first in wax that has been heated to about 93°C (200°F), and then in cold water, making sure the wick is not allowed to get wet. This will give the candle a good shine.

VARIATIONS ON DIPPED CANDLES
Twisted shapes

Take a candle that has been dipped to a thickness of, say, 3·8cm (1½in) and coloured,

but not allowed to harden. Lay the candle on a clean, flat surface, and roll it with a rolling pin, taking care not to allow the candle to stick to the surface. (If this happens, slide a knife gently under the candle and turn it over). Square the edges off by tapping gently. When the candle seems to be the correct thickness, twist the top and bottom gently in different directions until the desired shape is achieved. Then, hold the candle upright, tap the base until it is flat enough to stand upright. Plunge immediately into cold water and hold it there until it is completely hard. Take care not to remove the candle too soon. Wax retains its heat for a considerable time and though the outer surface may appear hard, the centre may still be soft. The candle will distort if removed too soon.

Plaited candles

With contrasting colours, the 'bucket and pipe' method of colouring can be employed. Cut suitable lengths of plastic drainpipe and put them into a bucket containing hot water. Then float different coloured molten waxes in each piece of drainpipe and maintain the temperature at 82°C (180°F). Using, say, three basic white candles and dipping in rotation, contrasting coloured candles can be made simultaneously.

When the candles are the required colour, and the outer surfaces have dried, they can be plaited together. This is much easier to do if you have someone to help by holding

the candles. If the candles harden before plaiting is completed, return them to their respective colours and dip a few times until they become malleable. See the picture on page 7 (top). Alternatively three candles can just be twisted together as shown on page 6.

Pear shaped candles
(Illustration page 7, bottom)

Another variation is to mould the candle in the hands while it is still warm, and vary the length of each dip. By dipping progressively less of the candle in the wax, a roughly pear shaped candle will form, which can be gently moulded by hand between each dipping until it is smooth. A final coat of colour can be added in the usual way.

Cut-back dips

It is also possible to build up layers of different colours, each one preferably at least 0·6cm (¼in) thick, as the colours will be exposed when the candle is finished. When several layers of colour have been added, the candle is allowed to harden. Then it is carved back to reveal the brilliant colours inside.

ROLLED BEESWAX SHEETS

Beeswax sheets are pre-formed sheets of pure beeswax, honeycombed in texture and varying in colour but usually found in an attractive creamy-yellow. As the sheets are malleable at room temperature, a candle can be rolled quite easily in a few minutes with-

out heating, pouring or waiting. In colder weather it may be necessary to hold the sheet over a heater for a few minutes to make it malleable.

To make a rolled beeswax candle, a clean flat surface must be used. Select a wick suitable for the diameter of the finished candle and cut the wick a few inches longer than the length of the beeswax sheet. Lay the wick along one edge of the sheet, and secure it by turning the sheet over to cover the wick. Then, as carefully and evenly as possible, roll the candle, always making sure that the base of the candle is level. When rolled, gently press the edge against the candle to prevent unrolling. Trim the wick to about 1·3cm ($\frac{1}{2}$in), and either dip the wick in molten beeswax, or pinch a small piece of beeswax sheet around the exposed wick to ensure that the wick is primed and ready to light.

For a pointed or tapered candle, the beeswax sheet must be prepared before rolling. Lay the square sheet on a cutting table and with a sharp knife and a ruler, cut off a triangular section from it. Beginning at the longest side of the remaining section, lay the wick and roll as before. To exaggerate the taper, cut a larger piece from the sheet, making one side very much shorter. At this stage, if different coloured beeswax sheeting is available, a two-tone effect can be achieved.

A straight candle can be decorated with small left over bits of beeswax sheet. (The middle candle on page 9, bottom).

Another idea for external decoration is to cut a sheet into strips and weave them together (illustrated page 9, top). The picture on page 9 (top) shows a whole group of beeswax candles. You will doubtless think up many variations of your own. Note that you can also cut the beeswax sheets into strips which you can then wrap round the candle (see page 9, bottom).

Small floating candles are easily made by making a small dish with two or three layers of beeswax sheet, and placing a rolled, tapered candle in the centre. These make attractive table or barbecue party decorations.

Any small pieces left over from beeswax sheets can be melted into a paraffin mixture to produce longer burning candles.

MOULDING
Moulding candles involves pouring wax into a leakproof mould. When the wax has hardened, and has taken the shape of that mould, the candle must either be removed from the mould, or the mould taken away from the candle.

Sand Moulding
Although sand-cast candles are one of the most unusual, we have started with this method of moulding, because it is in fact

9

Fig. 1

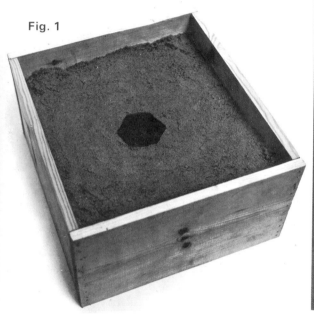

Fig. 2

the simplest, chiefly because sand is leak-proof and does not present the difficulties of many improvised moulds. A box or bucket of slightly damp sand (any kind of sand is suitable) is an ideal medium for moulding. Remember that the texture and colour of the sand will eventually be the outside surface of your candle. The surface of the sand should be levelled, but not compressed. Press a shape into the sand or, if a large candle is planned, scoop out some sand and then press a shape with a basin or similar object, making sure that the sand is not too tightly compressed. Remove the shape and smooth away any roughness you find in the sand. Once you have the basic shape, further variations can be made in it by pressing in the back of a spoon, the blade of a knife or a piece of shaped wood (see fig. 1, left).

The thickness of sand around the candle is controlled by the amount of moisture in the sand, which will prevent the wax spreading, and by the temperature of the

wax. Below 93°C (200°F), not much sand is picked up. It is impossible to heat wax above 100°C (212°F) with a double boiler. It is fool-hardy to heat wax above this temperature without using a thermometer.

Wax must never be heated over 350°F and it must always be heated gently because of its slow rate of heat transference. It cannot be stressed too emphatically that if you want a thick layer of sand on your candle and are therefore working at temperatures of above boiling point 100°C (212°F) great care must be taken. Before taking the wax from the heat, turn off the stove. Should wax ignite by accident, never attempt to put the fire out with water, because this will spread the wax. Stifle the flame with a saucepan lid or smother it with a damp cloth.

When the sand mould is prepared, carefully pour in your coloured candlewax, taking care not to disturb the design. Note that more wax will be needed than would normally fill the mould as a surprising

amount of wax is absorbed into the sand; it will also be necessary to top up.

When the surface of the candle has become rubbery, push a small hole for the wick into the centre of the candle with a knitting needle. It is effective to choose a smaller sized wick than would seem called for by the diameter of the candle, so on a 7·6cm (3in) diameter candle, choose a wick you'd normally use for a 5·1cm (2in) diameter candle. Your candle will then burn hollow, and if it is not left to burn for too long, the walls of the candle will remain in place. Dip the wick in hot wax, pull straight, allow to cool and insert it into the hole (pre-stiffened, lead-core wick is good for this).

As the candle cools the wax will contract forming a depression round the wick which has to be topped up with molten wax. To get a shiny top, keep topping up until the surface is flat, and cool it as swiftly as possible, even using a cold air fan. When the whole candle is completely set, dig it out of the sand. It will

look rather clumsy and shapeless as in fig. 2 on page 10. Finish by brushing off loose sand, and carve back to original shape with any kind of sharp tool or knife, until either the surface is smooth or the wax is exposed. The finished version of the candle on page 10 is shown on page 6. Loose sand on the outside surface can be fixed by immersing the walls of the candle in hot wax. The candle illustrated on page 10, top right, was made by this method.

Ready-made Moulds

Various craft shops sell different kinds of ready made moulds. The most common are rubber moulds. When using a rubber mould, choose a wick suitable for the diameter of the candle. Dip the wick in hot wax and pull it straight. Thread the wick through the mould with a wicking or any needle with a large eye, making sure that the wick is central. Tie the bottom end to a rod or a stick, pull top end tight and seal with mould seal (or any substitute like plasticine which is leak proof), being careful not to get any mould seal on the wick. Support the mould by hanging it from an improvised rack (see fig. 3, right) or support it between two pieces of wood, allowing the air to circulate around it. Don't support it in a box, as this will stop the air flow, nor in a water bath, as this tends to distort mould by pressure. To lengthen the life of rubber moulds, use a minimal amount of stearin when dissolving the dye—only about 1% instead of the usual 10% in proportion to the wax. Pour the coloured wax at 82°C (180°F), saving some for topping up. Tap the side of the mould lightly to remove trapped air bubbles. Leave until a well forms, and then break the sunken surface by prodding it with a stick. This will prevent the contracting wax from distorting the mould. Pour on more hot wax. Repeat until the surface is flat. If the mould sags, it can easily be reshaped by careful manipulation while it is still warm. Leave until it is cold. If you try to remove a candle from the mould while it is still warm, you might damage the candle. To release, rub the surface of the mould with soapy hands and warm water. Peel off carefully. Restore the mould to its original shape, wash and dry thoroughly and store away from heat and sunlight.

The matt candle surface can be polished by rubbing with hands or a soft cloth, and a small amount of beeswax in the candle mixture will make this much easier. Relief work can be highlighted by colouring with water-soluble paint mixed with a little soap, but do not use too much as paint will not burn and will clog the wick.

The candles on page 11 (top and bottom left) have been made with rubber moulds.

Metal moulds can also be bought ready-made, and are good because metal is an excellent heat conductor. It allows the candle to cool rapidly, and this, together with the smooth surface, leaves little finishing off to do. Make sure that the inside of the mould is clean; wax your chosen wick and secure it to a piece of stick. Thread the other end of the wick through the mould base, pull taut and seal with mould seal. Pour the prepared coloured candlewax into the mould at 88°C (190°F). If you wish to use perfume, add it immediately prior to pouring (according to maker's instructions), to ensure minimum evaporation.

Let the mould stand for a minute to allow air bubbles to rise, and lightly tap the mould to help them along. The texture of the finished candle can be varied, depending on the speed at which the wax is cooled. Rapid cooling with a water bath will produce an even finish. Slow cooling will result in what looks like air bubbles in the wax. A bucket or basin filled with cold water will serve as a cooling bath. The greater the volume of water, the faster the candle will

cool. Allow for the displacement of water when the mould is lowered. As the water level should be the same as the wax level, first try immersing the empty mould to ensure the right level of water. Don't pour wax into a mould that is already in a cooling bath—this will produce unsightly scales.

When all the air bubbles have risen and the mould is hot, lower it carefully into the cooling bath, making sure that no water enters the mould and that the level of the water is equal to the level of the wax in the mould (see fig. 4, page 13). You may have to weight the top of the mould to prevent it toppling over (see fig. 5). Let the candle cool, until a well begins to form. Break the surface skin and top up at 93°C (200°F), taking care not to overfill above the original level, as this would form a wedge and make mould release very difficult (see fig. 6). Allow candle to cool, invert the mould and slide the candle out. Trim the wick and level the base. The candles shown on page 12 have all been made from metal moulds.

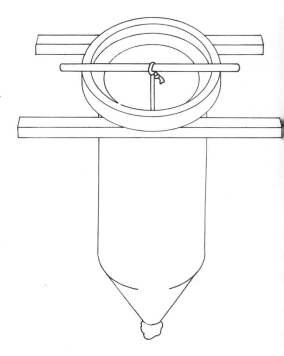

Fig. 3

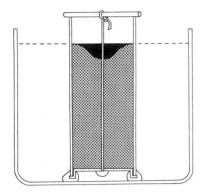

Fig. 4

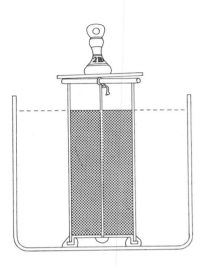

Fig. 5

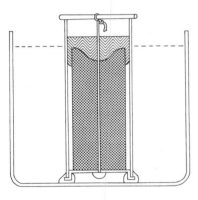

Fig. 6

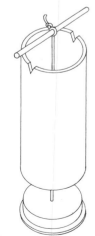

Fig. 7

Improvised Moulds

An infinite variety of moulds can be improvised. Many household containers, such as squeezy bottles, milk cartons, tins, yoghurt cartons, and food jars can be adapted—anything as long as the candle will come out easily when solidified. Other moulds can be made from cardboard, plastic drainpipe, rubber balls, balloons, acetate and PVC sheetings—it pays to experiment. Improvisation will lead to a few calamities, but wax can always be remelted and used again.

Having chosen your mould you must find a way of centralising the wick and keeping it taut in place. Figure 7 (below) shows a good way to secure the wick if an open-ended container is used. If you use a container with a fixed bottom or one in which you cannot bore a hole, the wick must be inserted after the candle has set. You can do this by drilling a hole (with an ordinary thin hand-drill), threading the wick and topping up with hot wax. Alternatively you can insert a needle or a skewer down the centre of the candle whilst it is still soft and pull it out once the wax has almost set and then insert the wick (as in sand-cast candles).

Whatever kind of mould you improvise, it is **most important** that the base is completely sealed before pouring in the wax. If it is not wax will ooze out and you will end up in a terrible mess! You can also embed your mould in sand, taking care not to get any sand inside the mould. Remember, too, that some plastics melt or soften with heat so do not use too hot wax. Also remember that you must never top up beyond the existing level of the candle as otherwise you will not only get an unsightly lip to the top of your candle but it will also prevent you from getting the candle out of the mould (see fig. 6).

All the candles on page 15 (top) were made from improvised moulds. The small cone-shape is made by casting whipped candlewax in layers in cardboard (see page 14). The larger blue cone next to it was

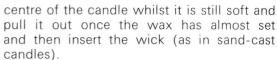

moulded in vinyl embossed wallpaper.

The strange blue candle was made by pouring wax into a piece of crumpled tin-foil containing crushed ice. The silver highlights are from pieces of foil which we left on an added decoration!

The red, green and white candle was made in a yoghurt carton with whipped wax (see page 14).

The square candle was made in a tea tin with left over yellow and white chunks which had been cooled very quickly and molten paraffin wax poured over them cooled slowly. The whole candle was then ironed back with a hot blade (see page 16).

The green candle was cast in a piece of convoluted hose from a car accessory shop.

The small candle was made from red and purple chunks moulded in a glass mustard pot. The diffused colour effect was obtained by dipping the mustard pot into hot water and then immersing in cold water. The mustard pot had to be broken to get the candle out.

The red and white candle was moulded in a piece of corrugated PVC sheeting with white whipped candlewax. Whilst the wax was still mouldable a piece of dowelling was pushed against the convex portions and the mould topped up with red molten candlewax.

The sphere was made in a rubber ball with the three colours of whipped wax. A hole was cut in the top of the ball. The ball was then cut in half and stuck together again with sticky tape. This enabled us to remove the candle easily and re-use the mould.

The method of making the coloured white candle is described under 'whisking' on page 14. It was moulded in PVC sheeting which was scored and folded into shape.

The bunch of grapes on page 14 (top left) was made by pouring candlewax into refrigerator ice trays and sticking the bunch round a wick (see page 16).

TEXTURES AND TECHNIQUES
Multilayered candles
(illustration page 11)
These are made by pouring different coloured waxes into a mould at different times. A layer of wax is poured at 82°C (180°F) and allowed to cool until the surface is rubbery. The next colour is then poured gently onto the first, again at 82°C (180°F), and this is left to set to the same rubbery surface. The layers are thus built up, and the candle is finally topped up when the well has appeared (see fig. 8 page 16). By simply standing the mould at an angle, layers can be built up diagonally (see fig. 9).

Chunks
Fill a mould with chunks of left-over wax of many colours, and pour white or coloured paraffin wax over the chunks in a mould at 93°C (200°F). It is advisable to use a cooling bath to prevent the chunks colouring

the molten wax too much. The candle below left has been made in this way and the white wax carved back with a wax knife or ordinary penknife to reveal the colours inside.

Ice Candles
On the same principle, put crushed ice into a mould, pour the wax over the ice, and place the mould immediately into the cooling bath. The ice will melt and when the wax has hardened, the candle can be removed and the water poured away. It is very important to use a thin candle already wicked as the central core because water on the wick will spoil the burning of the candle (picture page 13, centre).

Whisking
If you have some cooling candlewax, you can whisk it with a fork or egg-whisker to make a frothy, meringue-like mixture with a completely different texture. As this mixture needs a much lower temperature than the usual wax, it allows the use of mould materials that would lose their shape at normal pouring temperatures (i.e. 82°–93°C (190°–200°F)). But remember, when using wax at these lower temperatures, it will not contract as much, so you must pick a suitable mould.

The whipped mixture is poured or spooned into the prepared mould and packed firmly down to prevent cavities. Different coloured whipped waxes can be packed into the same mould, producing marbled effects (the candles moulded with whipped wax on page 15, top). If you are using a transparent mould, it is possible to draw designs on your candle. Powdered dye can be transferred to the surface of the candle by pushing it on the end of a thin stick through the centre of the candle, thus dying a pattern on the wax from the inside. Additional whipped wax can be used to seal in the dye. To finish the candle, a thin layer of molten wax is poured at 71°C (160°F) to seal the surface. Whipped wax can also be used as a decoration on ordinary moulded candles, or it can be moulded by hand into a particular shape. White whipped wax, for example, can be hand-moulded into a snowball.

BALLOON CANDLES
See illustration on page 15
Partly fill a round balloon with cold water until the balloon reaches the required diameter, say 5·1cm (2in) to 7·6cm (3in). Heat some paraffin wax to 77°C (170°F) and repeatedly dip the balloon (which must be dried properly first) into it up to the same level each time. Repeat about ten times, allowing a 30 second interval between each dip for the coats to harden. When the last coat has hardened, carefully let the water out of the balloon. It should pull away from the inner surface of the shell and fall out.

Expect a high failure rate of fragile shells!

Now heat a small quantity of stearin and dye. If you want several colours, put, say, three cups in a pan of boiling water and dissolve a tablespoonful of stearin and a generous amount of dye in each cup. When the dye has dissolved, add one tablespoonful of paraffin wax to each colour. The colour must be strong. Put a teaspoonful or less into the shell, and immediately rotate the shell very quickly, rather as if it were a glass of brandy. Empty out any wax that has not adhered, as the thin shell will soon distort if a pool of wax is allowed to remain static. Repeat this process until the inside of the shell is decorated. Cool quickly, by blowing or with a cold air fan. Even a finger's pressure will form a depression, so speed is essential.

Paraffin wax must now be added, a tablespoonful at a time; as you add each tablespoonful of wax at 99°C (190°F), the shell must be rotated, so that the wax coat can adhere. Any excess must be poured at once into the wax pot, for again no pools of hot wax can be allowed in the shell.

Continue slowly filling until a wall, 1·3cm ($\frac{1}{2}$in) thick, of wax has built up. Do not leave the shell resting on a hard surface at any time until you are sure the wax is hard. Small quantities of paraffin wax can now be poured in and allowed to cool, but again, this must not be rushed. When the shell is

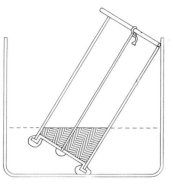

Fig. 8

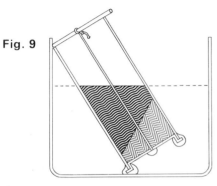

Fig. 9

¾ full, drill a hole for the wick in the centre. Top up the candle. It is worth adding 5 to 10% of beeswax to this kind of candle, to give it longer burning time.

FINISHING TECHNIQUES

Almost any candle can be enhanced by a good finish. For instance, a sharp hammer tap will leave a bruise mark on the surface of a candle, which can be used to build up a pattern (illustration page 13, right). Variations on chunk candles can be achieved by cutting back the clear wax to expose the rough surface of the coloured chunks. After this, dip in hot wax at 99°C (210°F) or hot water, to round off rough edges. You can also 'iron back' a surface with a heated large-bladed knife or spatula, working on a tray to catch the drips. Coloured pieces of wax can be stuck on the outside of a candle. Pour a thin sheet of strongly dyed wax into a tray and let it harden. When set, break or carve it into pieces. Press a hot knife blade onto the surface of the candle, and place a piece of wax on the blade. Slide the knife away, welding the two wax surfaces together. This is best done on a white candle to give maximum glow. Different coloured wax can also be dripped, painted or written onto a candle with either a brush or tjanting pen, using strongly dyed beeswax (see bottom picture page 12).

The Candles on page 6

You will recognise most of the candles illustrated on page 6. The red 'rocket' candle was made by placing pieces of triangular glass in sand, to make a star shape.

The tall cone-shaped candle shows one effect of layering. The cone mould was made out of a plain piece of cardboard. The brown and gold candles were both made from ready-made moulds and show how the relief work can be high-lighted with a little paint. The large pink candle was made in a 10·2cm (4in) plastic drainpipe and hammered when hard. For the cylindrical candle the 'balloon' method was used.

FAULT CHART

Fault	Cause	Remedy
Dipping		
Lumpy surface on candle	Dipped too cold	Dip candle in wax at 93°C (200°F)
Candle spits whilst burning	Water in candle	Pour off the molten wax in candle, relight If this is not successful, remelt
White marks in layers of cut back dipped candles	Dipped too cold	A quick dip in wax at 93°C (200°F) may be successful
Candle cracks while plaiting or rolling	Uneven temperature throughout candle; i.e. the centre may be harder than the surface of the candle	Redip until the candle is completely pliable
Scum forms on the surface when floating wax on water	Impurities or dirty wax	Ladle off surface scum, make sure you still have at least 1½in (3·8cm) of molten wax
Moulding		
Leaking mould, from base	Careless wicking up	Seal with mould seal
Misshapen candle (rubber mould)	Badly supported mould, or not topped up regularly enough	If candle has set too much and cannot be gently shaped by rolling candle in hands, remelt
Air bubbles on surface of candle	Candle not tapped soon after pouring to release air bubbles	Extra care taken in finishing, using water soluble paints can cover bad surface
Scaly marks on surface of candle	Wax poured too cold (usually below 77°C (170°F))	Remelt, although a dip in hot molten wax (93°C (200°F)) may improve the finish
Large cracks throughout the candle	Thermal cracks, candle cooled too rapidly; i.e. in a refrigerator or in wintry conditions	Remelt or use as chunks
Candle will not come out of mould	Insufficient stearic acid used; or the candle has been topped up above the original level, causing a wedge between candle and mould; or slow cooling resulting in less contraction and difficult mould release	Place mould in hot water and melt candle out
Loss of definition with layered candles	Previously poured wax not set sufficiently to support the next layer. The surface should be rubbery. Pour layers at 82°C (180°F)	Remelt, remember the resulting wax will be a combination of colours, usually brown
Base colour poured over chunks changes colour	Wax poured too hot, pour at 93°C (200°F)	Carve away discoloured wax
Whipped wax doesn't take the shape of the mould	Air trapped by whipped wax. Always pack the wax tightly into mould, or tap the filled mould on a flat surface	Remelt, or a dip into hot wax may be used as an effective remedy
Layers not joining	Wax poured too late at too low a temperature. Always pour onto a rubbery surface at 82°C (180°F)	Remelt or chunk up
Layers seeping between candle and mould	Wax allowed to set completely and contracting away from the side of the mould allowing some of the next layer to seep down the side	Cut off the unwanted marks, and dip in hot uncoloured wax at 99°C (210°F). This may improve the finish
Small bubbly line encircling candle	Level of cooling bath lower than the level of the wax in the mould	Remelt, use as chunks or hammer
Small pit marks on the surface of the candle	Air bubbles not allowed to rise before placing in a cooling bath	Next time allow 1 minute before placing mould in cooling bath
Beeswax sheets begin to crack when rolling	Although beeswax is extremely flexible, in cold conditions it may sometimes crack	Place in front of fan heater or similar to warm sheets before rolling
Shell cracks when making 'shell' candles	Wax cooling too fast causing thermal cracks, or a too high melting point used	Remelt, try again
Shell misshapen when removing shell from balloon	Shells not cooled sufficiently before removing from balloon. Hot wax not poured from shell or not kept in motion	Remelt, try again

16

Batik

CREATING A BATIK

A batik is not a painting on a piece of material; it is a pattern or picture dyed into a piece of cloth. The method consists in preparing certain parts of the material so that they will not take the dye.

The basic tone of the material (usually silk or linen) is white, or a pastel colour. Certain areas of the material are covered with hot liquid wax using a tjanting (batiking tube) or a brush; the wax permeates and seals the parts it covers so that the dye cannot penetrate. The material is then dipped into a dye bath—the first colour being the lightest tone of those to be used. Next, those areas which are to retain the colour just dyed are covered with wax, and the material is dipped into a dye of a colour darker in tone than the first. This process continues until the darkest shade (black) has been reached. Since the colours are superimposed in the dyeing process, a particular colour-scale must be adhered to. For example, if the first dye is red and the second blue, keep in mind that the end result is not blue but violet.

After the last dyeing, the material is dried and placed between two layers of absorbent paper (such as old newsprint). The wax is ironed out of the material and into the paper. When all the wax has been ironed out, the batik reveals the pattern or picture that has been permanently dyed into the cloth. This is always an exciting moment, for one can never be sure of having achieved a perfect separation of the colours—a good result depends on this.

Characteristic of this process are the cracks or breaks in the design. Congealed wax is hard and brittle; thus it happens that during the dyeing or rinsing of the material, the wax cracks and the dye penetrates these places. This results in the fine spiderweb pattern which lends batik its peculiar charm, giving it a life of its own.

This very old technique originated in Indonesia; the island of Java still produces exquisite materials and wall hangings decorated by this process, richly ornamented, and very often of the highest artistic merit.

WHAT IS BATIK?
Preliminary Sketch (Choice of Motif)

Make a preliminary sketch to start with. Begin with simple motifs, such as patterns consisting of lines, dots, squares, circles, flowers, trees, animals, houses. In this chapter a great variety of motifs are illustrated, from the simplest to the more complex. The best way is to make a charcoal

17

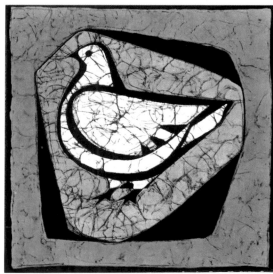

Fig. 1

Fig. 2

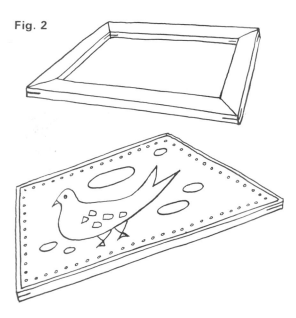

Stretching the Material on the Frame and transferring the Sketch to the Material.

sketch on paper. Mistakes can be rectified easily by erasing with a soft cloth. Suppose we do a tapestry, such as 'the dove' (above). The size will depend on the size of the frame on which we mount our piece of material. We can also scale the frame to fit the material; in any case, the preliminary sketch must be of the same size as the project. We must now decide upon a colour scheme.

For 'the dove', we choose three colours, pink, blue and black. The material receiving the batik is white. The material is stretched on an old picture frame, or on a canvas stretcher, with the help of thumb tacks. The design is either traced onto the material or sketched on direct.

When we have finished our sketch, we prepare the frame on which we stretch the material. We can use an old picture frame, or a canvas stretcher which can be obtained in any art materials store. The advantage of this last is that it can be easily fitted together and taken apart, or its size altered. Stretch the material to be batiked on the frame, using thumb tacks. Take care that the material is smoothly and evenly stretched: it must lie taut while the wax is being applied

or it will stick to the working surface.

The choice of a particular material depends on the use the batik is destined for. For example: for shawls, head scarves, blouse material—in short, for articles of fashion—we use pure silk, or Japanese raw silk, and sometimes fine cotton. For tapestries, tablecloths, banners and so on, we choose finetextured Japanese raw silk, fine linen, batiste, cotton, or grasscloth.

It is very important that materials are not dyed, that is, they must be white or natural. Materials that have been finished or glazed must first of all be washed in soap and water or in a soda-solution. Finished or dressed material will not take dyes at all well. Now that we have our chosen material on the frame we proceed with the transference of the design. This can be done in various ways: take a piece of transparent paper, place it over the sketch and trace the design with India ink. Now pin or tape the traced pattern underneath the framed piece of material and place this on a sheet of glass which may be smaller (but of course not larger) than the frame. When this is lit up with a lamp, the design can be clearly seen through the material. Now we can easily trace the design onto the fabric with a soft pencil (see fig. 1, top left). Since these lines will disappear after repeated dyebaths, especially if we have used charcoal for sketching, it is a good idea to block out all the traced lines with the tjanting at the time of the first wax application.

This manner of transference is employed only in the case of closely woven or thick fabric. To trace designs onto transparent, thin fabrics, we simply place the design on a light-coloured surface with the material on top, and trace the design as described above.

We can also sketch the design directly onto the material using pencil or charcoal. This is the quickest method for anyone who has had a little experience in drawing.

Fig. 3

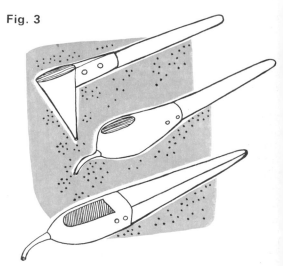

Three types of tjanting.

Fig. 4

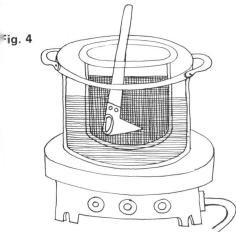

This drawing shows the hotplate and the two containers—one for the water and inside it another one for the wax. The tjanting (batiking tube) is shown in the wax pot.

APPLYING THE WAX

We are now ready to begin the batik. To melt the wax, we need a hotplate, a pot that fits well on it (for the water) and a smaller pot (preferably copper) with a handle, in which to melt the wax. (A set of pots for such purposes, made of copper, is commercially available). Zinc pots should *not* be used for melting wax, but enamel pots are fine.

Now melt beeswax in combination with paraffin (three parts wax to one part paraffin); the water must be kept boiling softly, even while the work of application goes on. Now dip the tjanting into the hot wax, scoop up a small amount, and block out the outlines of the design, that is, those parts of the dove which are to remain white. (In this case, use a flat rather wide brush to apply the wax.) If the wax has not penetrated everywhere, turn the frame over and apply wax where necessary. Mistakes made at this stage cannot be corrected, for it is impossible to remove the wax so that the dye will take. In case of errors it is best to start again.

Tjantings can be had in different sizes to produce thin or thick lines. When blocking out, be sure not to take too much wax at a time (the wax hardens very fast). Prevent unwanted dripping by holding a piece of cloth under the tjanting when bringing it over the material. It is important, then, to apply the wax as speedily as possible, and as soon as it begins to harden return the tjanting to the pot and wait until it heats up again, and so on.

DYEING

When we have blocked out the part of the design that is to remain white, we begin with the dyeing. For our design, we begin with pink. As has been said, the dyeing process always proceeds step by step from the lightest to the darkest colour. Use textile inks available in arts and craft stores, or ordinary fabric dyes. For lighter or darker tones, use more or less water. Prepare the dye in plastic or enamel bowl, large enough to

permit the batik to be submerged easily and moved about. Use warm water, up to 90°F (32°C), but no hotter or the wax will melt. Dissolve packet of dye in a small enamel container in about half a pint of boiling water and pour it into the warm water through a piece of used linen cloth. This prevents undissolved particles of dye from entering the solution. Now mix the solution well. We are now ready to dye. Take the batik from the frame, dip it into plain water first, then into the dye. For the dipping, use two wooden sticks; or better, wear rubber gloves. Recently many cold fast dyes have been developed which are, of course, more practical and which are usually widely available. If not, you will have to use the traditional methods of dyeing.

Dyeing takes from five to twenty minutes, or until the desired shade (in this case, of pink) is reached. Bear in mind that the wet fabric shows stronger colouring than the dry. We can get a fair idea of the shade by removing the batik from the dyebath and holding it up to a window or a light. When the desired shade is reached, remove the batik from the dye and rinse it in cold water—do not wring. It is this rinsing that causes the cracks characteristic of batik. The wax cracks and thus admits dye during subsequent colouring; these places can be blocked out with wax again, but not before the last colouring.

Now let the batik drip dry, and stretch it on the frame once more. When it is completely dry, we block out again, this time all the areas that are to retain the pink colour, that is, as can be seen in fig. 1, top right and bottom left. Now we prepare the blue dye; all areas that have not been blocked out will now take on this colour. Leave the batik in the dye long enough so that the pink is completely covered, i.e. until a deep shade of blue is reached.

Method of Removing Colour

If, for example, we had dyed a deep red instead of pink, and then wished to use also a strong blue or green, we would first have to use a colour remover; for blue on red produces purple. In this case we would have to treat the batik in a bath of colour-remover. This would remove the red colour from all areas not treated with wax. After this process, rinse the batik well. Now the blue could be dyed.

Waxed areas that are put through several dyebaths should be recoated where they appear too thin between the dyeing. In the case of thick fabrics (such as linen), coat the back of the material as well to make sure of good coverage.

After the first wax-blocking, we can also apply any colour we choose with a brush, without dipping the batik into a dye (see page 19, top and bottom). We must, however, use a concentrated colour-solution, not the ordinary solution for the dyebath. This is recommended for small areas of colour that have already been blocked out. Also, this method can only be used where the batik will not have to be washed; through the application of such concentrated colour the material becomes saturated and may bleed when washed. This method, then, can only be used in the case of wall-hangings or banners which will not be washed later. Once we have applied concentrated dye with a brush we block out the areas with wax and continue the dyeing process as described above.

After blocking out all areas that are to retain the blue colour on our batik, we are ready to dye the last and darkest shade we are using—black. In the course of the foregoing dyebaths and rinsings many cracks and thin areas will have appeared. Some of these places should now be re-waxed, to prevent too much of the next colour from coming through. All remaining areas not blocked out now receive the darkest shade in our colour-scheme—black.

Removing the Wax

After the last dyeing, the batik is well rinsed and dried. Now we remove the wax by ironing the batik between sheets of old newsprint or blotting paper. Keep changing the sheets until all the wax has been absorbed. Do not use newspapers; the fresh printer's ink would transfer to the material, and could not be completely removed again. It is also possible to remove the wax with hot water. The last remaining traces of wax are removed with cleaning fluid. This should be done outdoors, if possible, for the fluid is very inflammable. The batik may be squeezed out gently in the cleaning fluid, then hung

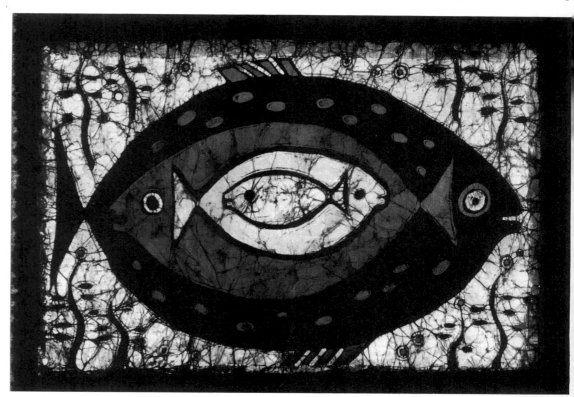

up to dry. Save the fluid for future use—the wax sinks to the bottom. Use a (plastic) gallon container with a good seal to store the fluid. Our batik is now finished (see fig. 1, lower right).

Wall Hanging for Children's Room (top)
Material: white linen (20 × 24in)
Colours dyed were yellow, light brown, and black. The finished batik was embroidered in small areas with gold thread.

Wall Hanging: Fish within Fish (centre)
Material: batiste (16 × 26in)
The fabric is white. In this case the white areas were thinly blocked out, and after the first dyeing (pink) and the second dyeing (pale blue) the wax was re-applied to the white areas. This results in the delicate pink and blue tones in the white. The pink must be dyed lightly so that it is covered by the blue which follows; if the pink is too dark, the blue turns violet.

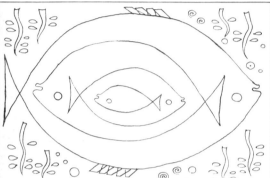

Step-by-step procedure:
1. sketch on material,
2. white blocked out, pink dyed, blocked out,
3. blue dyed, blocked out,
4. last dyeing, black.

Wall Hanging: Edge of the Forest
(bottom)
Material: Japanese raw silk (8 × 48in)
The colour of the material is ivory; the dyed colours are pink and black. Blocking out was done solely with the janting, which resulted in a particularly striking effect in the structure of the individual areas and breaks. This method is usable only if small areas are being blocked out. It is also much more time-consuming than working with the brush.

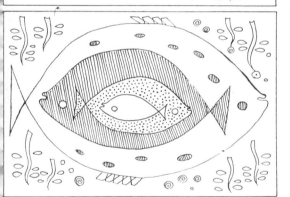
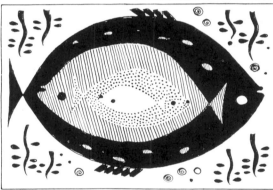

Wall Hanging: Child on a Pony
(page 19, bottom)
Material: white linen
Colours dyed are light blue and black. All the other colours, i.e. ruby red, light brown and cornflower blue were applied (mixed in various concentrations) with a brush before the first (light blue) dyeing and blocked out upon drying. Make sure that the areas painted in with the brush are surrounded by thin lines free of wax, so that the colour which has slightly diffused around the edges of the design will be covered up during the last dyeing (black).

Wall Hanging: The Parade (page 19, top)
Material: white linen
Dyed with light brown, light pink, scarlet red and black. The light blue, aquamarine blue, and violet were applied with a brush before the first dyeing (pink) and blocked out along with basic colour (white). Proceed as above.

Table Cover (White Material) *(above)*
Two colours were used here, first red, then emerald green. The two colours combine to produce a dark blue. The design was created from interlocking circles, traced onto the material with the help of a circle cut from cardboard. The white areas were first blocked out using a bristle brush; after the first dyeing the red areas were blocked out.

Wall Hanging: Sunflower *(right)*
Material: white silk (32 × 32in)
Colours: red-orange and black

STAMPED BATIK OR TJAP-PRINT
The wax can also be applied with a stamp, as in potato-printing. Stamps can be fashioned from wood or bamboo sticks. The material is stretched on the frame as usual, the stamp is dipped into the liquid wax, applied to the material and immediately removed again. To prevent dripping, hold a piece of cloth or cardboard under the stamp. After each printing the stamp must be dipped into the wax anew. The pattern is created by the juxtaposition of these stamped designs. If we should wish to dye in two colours we must leave enough room during the first printing to allow for a second one, after the first dyeing.

Tritik Technique *(left)*
This method stems from Java and means, basically, 'sowing, folding, knotting'. Materials needed are cloth, needle, thread, twine, and colours.
From the middle of the piece of cloth, gather up a spiral, using needle and strong thread. Pull the thread tight, and wind the gathered piece of cloth with the remaining thread and then with a length of waxed twine. Now place the roll of cloth into the dyebath, afterwards dipping the two ends briefly into another colour. Remove twine and thread, dry and iron the finished piece.

DRIP BATIK
This kind of batik is done on white, dyed first yellow, then blue. The finished product is white-yellow-green. For this very simple technique we need only a candle, a frame, thumb tacks and two colours of dye. Stretch the material on the frame, drip wax from a burning candle (start in the middle) in tight circles, proceeding towards the edges of the fabric, making circles wider and wider. Remove the cloth from frame and dip for a few minutes into the lighter (here yellow) of the two dyes. Rinse in vinegar solution, and let dry. When the batik is completely dry, repeat the process, drip wax in between first drops. Then dye the darker colour (in this case, blue). Areas with no wax will come out green. Iron the wax out of the batik between sheets of newsprint or tissue paper.

Working with Metal Foils

From the earliest times men have admired the brilliance of precious stones and metals. The same delight in colour and contrast is evident in the art of the Baroque and Rococo periods which filled European churches with ornate figures adorned with gold beads and lace.

The more austere designs favoured today have their place, but not everyone can delight in them. Shops are full of attractive gifts, but sometimes we think how much more our friends would appreciate gifts that we have made ourselves. Here we show you what you can do inexpensively and simply.

As you will quickly find, experimenting with new and exciting ideas is enjoyable as well as productive.

The things suggested in the following pages depend largely for their construction and decoration on the use of metal-foil, sequins and beads. Metal foil is very easy to work with, and can be bent, folded and painted, as well as imprinted and embossed.

Metal-foil stamping

A picture or ornamental design imprinted on the foil attractively exploits the natural beauty of its surface by creating a variety of planes that enrich the interplay of light and shade. For this kind of work, the foil should be placed on a flat, soft surface such as cardboard, linoleum, or newspaper.

You can use either the conventional stencil and tracing instruments, blunt knitting-needles or discarded ball-point pens. For lines of particular depth and breadth, you will need such instruments as, for example, the ball stylus and ruling-wheel pen supplied by Gestetner.

Neo-foil can be used to produce durable decorative items on which strong ornamental relief patterns can be worked. A drop of oil should first be rubbed over the foil as this makes for greater ease when tools are run across its surface.

A ruler or set-square is used when making geometrical patterns (for example, the match-boxes on page 24). For free patterns or drawings, as well as for letters of the alphabet (especially for one's first efforts), it is best to make a drawing on tracing-paper and then to transfer it lightly on to the foil. Make sure that the surface you rest the foil on is perfectly flat.

If the letters are to stand out in bold relief, then they must be impressed on the reverse side of the foil, and inscribed in mirror writing (right to left, with letters in reverse). First efforts are best done on foil scraps until you have gained the confidence and ease that come with practice.

The bold relief of such patterns can be strengthened by adding Polyfilla, for example, or Plasticine to the grooves on the reverse side.

Circles are made with a pair of dividers, while lines for folding (indicated in the diagrams by———) are impressed with a soft pencil or stylus, taking care to apply only a light pressure to thin foil so as to avoid breaking. Another way is to fold the foil over the edges of the box.

Foil-painting

Painting adds a special charm to the foil. Silver foil is best (see the match-box page 26, top). In fact, all metal-foils are originally silver-foils which have been tinted gold, red, blue and so on, with transparent colours. You can give the silver-foil any colour you wish while retaining its metallic gleam by using transparent metal colours. You will need only the basic colours of yellow, red and light blue, which you can mix on the silver foil to produce a wide range of colours. For example, a mixture of yellow and blue will give violet.

Thinners or nail-polish removers can be used as cleaners and paint removers, but remember to follow the directions for use. It is especially important to clean the paint-brushes after use.

Impress the drawing or pattern on the foil first, so that the paints in the separate areas of colour are prevented from mixing by the grooves between them. If a line or pattern is to stand out in silver from the coloured background, it should be embossed by working from the reverse side of the foil. After you have finished painting, this relief-pattern can be wiped with a small rag (or with a drop of paint-remover, if necessary).

Paint dries quickly on foil, and other colours can be added quickly to produce interesting tones of colour. Different shades and tones of colour can also be produced by adding colours to coloured foil. For example, blue paint on gold-foil produces green; yellow added to gold-foil gives a powerful brass-lustre such as you can see on the cigarette-box (page 26, top) and on the match-box (page 28, bottom).

Transparent and opaque colours can be mixed to produce interesting colour-tones, while the addition of white and coloured nail-lacquers (ordinary and pearlised) can create an effect that suggests the colours are flowing into each other. A wide range of colour-effects is open to anyone who is willing to experiment like this.

Flat colour contrasts

An interesting combination is presented by adding a flat colour (black poster-colour, for example) to the gleam of the foil. The foil is laid on a flat, smooth surface and fixed firmly with drawing pins or adhesive tape before painting evenly with a good bristle-brush. After the first coat has dried, a second coat may also be applied, and when perfectly dry, the work may be polished with a soft rag or cotton-wool.

Exposed silver patterns

Where paint has been added to the foil, interesting patterns may be produced by scraping off the paint with a knitting needle or scraper-blade.

Similar patterns can be made on the ordinary lacquered foil by scraping lightly with a scraper-blade so that the underlying silver is exposed to present a strong pattern that seems to glisten against the overall colour of the foil. The picture on the right shows an example of this in the match-box holder (top left-hand corner).

Pattern emphasis

After impressing the pattern into foil laid on a smooth, flat surface, the foil is brushed with black poster-colour which is allowed to dry for only a short time before being carefully rubbed off with a damp piece of cloth or very fine sandpaper. The black that remains in the grooves of the pattern causes it to stand out more effectively against the foil background.

Adhesive

Experience has shown that for lacquered or painted foils Bostik No. 1 is best since it does not dissolve the colour. For Styrofoam balls the ammonia-based fabric adhesive is suitable, while for glass, Bostik No. 1 can also be used.

Casting

Many of the articles will have a base made from plaster of Paris, such as the candle-

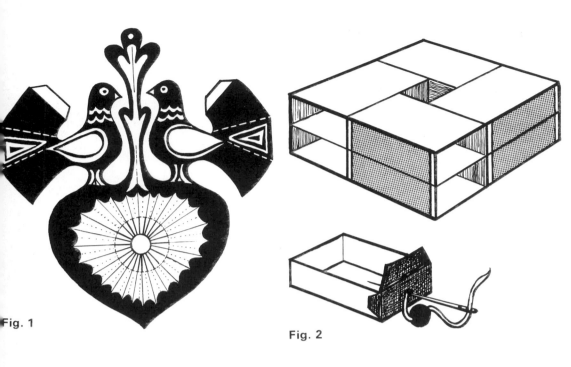

Fig. 1

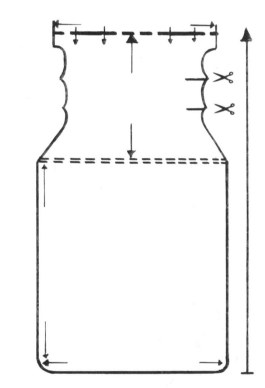

Fig. 2

holder shown on page 26, top, the foil-blossom tree on page 27, top left, and the pin-cushions on page 31. Used plastic containers of food, drink and cosmetics are best for casting since they are pliable enough not to crack as the plaster expands while setting. However, if glass or clay containers are used as moulds, then it is better to use Polyfilla. Both these materials are mixed in a can and used immediately. Plaster of Paris in particular sets very quickly, so remember to insert central needles or dowelling rods without delay.

Materials and equipment

Whatever you need for this craft may be obtained from stationers and hobby-shops, and so on. Haberdashers supply sequins, beads and ribbon; florists supply wire and Styrofoam balls. It is advisable to limit yourself to two or three colours that can be used for various crafts. In addition, you should lay in a small stock of the following materials: coloured foil or cellophane sweet wrappers (as used in making Garden of Eden shown on page 30, top, and the trinket box on page 26, bottom), silver paper, cooking foil, tinfoil, foil-lids or bottle-caps, cake-cups, trimmings, small boxes and cosmetic containers. Christmas is a good time for collecting things that can be purchased only then, such as small balls in gold, silver and red, tinsel and silver and gold thread (i.e. Christmas tree decorations) all of which you can turn to good account in your craft-work.

You will also need a small pair of scissors, pointed tweezers, two fine paint brushes (Nos. 1 and 2), and one broad bristle-brush.

HEART AND SUN-FISH

The heart is shown in colour on page 23. These decorations are intended primarily

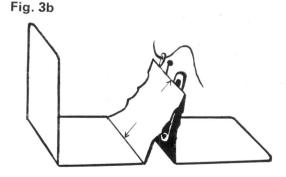

Fig. 3a

Fig. 3b

for hanging. They can also be used for Christmas tree decorations, and smaller versions of them may be used as tags on gift-parcels for your friends.

HEART

The heart-and-dove shape (see fig. 1) is drawn on silver foil. The extra flap on the doves is to give a fantail effect to the finished decoration. After you have cut the outline and impressed the foil, paint on the heartshape with transparent yellow paint. Then after cutting the outline of the inner heart from red foil, impress the out-going rays, while making sure that the short, inner rays are cut from the centre outwards, and opened outwards, before being fixed with adhesive, as shown in the diagram. A glittering spangle is fixed in the middle of its central opening. Finally, the leaf is cut and formed from green foil, and then fixed. The effect is even more attractive if both faces of the decoration are worked in the same way, before hanging with a thread.

SUN-FISH

Choose a picture of an attractive-looking sun fish from any good natural history book. After drawing the outline of a fish on silver foil and cutting it out, impress the eyes and scales before painting on both sides. This may be done in different colours: for example, the front could be painted blue and the back red. Cut two discs out of gold foil for the sun, paint them transparent yellow, and fix to both sides of the fish.

LARGE MATCH-BOXES

The lower left-hand corner of the picture on page 24 shows only one of many possibilities. This box has foil stuck to the upper face only. The foil is cut exactly to size, and with the help of a ruler the geometric pattern is impressed on it. With care, even the beginner will find this kind of pattern quite easy.

If the box is to have foil all over it, it is best to cover it with paper first, and from this the required piece of foil can be marked and cut before folding it carefully around the box in order to determine where the strike surfaces come. These areas are then cut out of the foil, starting very carefully from a slit in the middle so that the scissors have enough room to manoeuvre and can cut accurately along the fold lines. The upper side is then worked into an attractive pattern before folding the foil around the box and gluing the end flaps in position. By taking the drawer from a new box of matches, this box can be used over and over again.

The illustration on page 26, top, shows a match-box cover made from silver aluminium-foil. Not only the house and trees were impressed and printed, but the ends of the foil and the borders of the striking surface were embossed and painted.

The match-box cover illustrated on page

28, bottom, is made from brass-foil. The first step is to impress the outline of the rectangle and then to inscribe the circle with a pair of dividers. The outer area is decorated with strokes and dots as shown; the central monogram stands out in raised relief by carefully working from the reverse side of the foil. Finally, the pattern is painted in with transparent yellow.

The brass-foil cover on the cigarette-container shown on the left was also made in this way (detailed directions, page 27).

SMALL MATCH-BOXES

Figure 2, page 25 shows how one can use a collection of small boxes to ensure an adequate and attractive source of supply.

The only materials needed are 8 match-boxes, 2 squares of foil measuring 12×12cm ($4\frac{3}{4} \times 4\frac{3}{4}$in), 2 squares of cardboard measuring 9×9cm ($3\frac{1}{2} \times 3\frac{1}{2}$in), 8 glass beads (four black and four white), and black adhesive tape.

The eight boxes (drawers removed) are glued together as shown in fig. 2, page 25 (striking surfaces outwards!). One of the cardboard squares is covered with one of the foil squares and glued on as a base. The second foil square is worked with a pattern to cover the upper surface. We used red foil with a flower and diagonal pattern, as shown on page 24, bottom. The diagonals were embossed, while the flowers were first impressed with the dividers and then worked in continuous lines, or in dots as shown. An effective touch is to scratch out small parts of the pattern so that the silver under-layer stands out in contrast with the red.

The patterned foil is then fitted over the other cardboard square and glued to the top-side. The black adhesive tape is attached to the front of the match box drawers as shown below. After fixing the bead in position with a large darning-needle and twine (knotted inside the drawer), the flap of adhesive tape is pressed down on the inside of the drawer front. Put the matches back in the drawers, and there you are.

SMALL NEEDLE-CASE

This is a simple project for someone, who, with little time, would like to give a friend a useful gift. Though not much larger than a book of matches it can hold thread, needles, safety pins, buttons and press-studs. It makes an invaluable 'emergency kit', and will fit into the smallest handbag.

All that is needed is a strip of foil 24×5cm ($9\frac{1}{2} \times 2$in), good drawing paper, and about four darning needles, 2 safety-pins, black, brown and white thread, small buttons and press-studs.

Working with thick foil, you can mark off the measurements which are shown in figs. 3a and b, on the foil and then cut and fold. Using thin foil, however, it would be advisable to cut the outline from the drawing

10.XI. 1966

HERTHA WITZEMANN

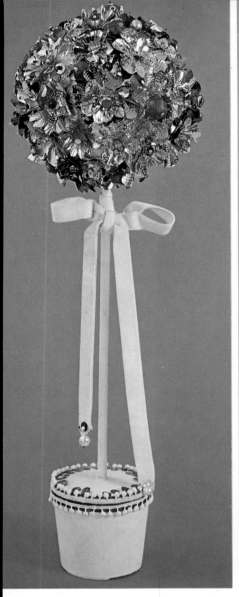

paper and then cover it inside and out with the foil. The front flap should have a simple pattern or your friend's initials worked on it. The scalloped middle part is then folded and the threads are wound lightly round the separate scallops, the needles and the safety-pins are inserted from the top, and button and press-stud-cards are fixed with adhesive to the flaps.

BOOK OF MATCHES
All that is needed to make the match-book covers shown on page 24 is a strip of foil or double-faced gold-paper measuring 21 × 5cm (9 × 2in) to fold without adhesive around the book of matches. Because of its firmness and flexibility, it will be available for other books of matches as the old one is finished. The front flap can carry a simple pattern, initial-letter, or a large circular splash of colour.

BOOK JACKETS
We may often make presents of pocket-books, and by adding a thick foil jacket, patterned, or with recipient's initials in-scribed, the gift will be appreciated all the more. The jacket also provides a durable cover for the book. A carefully worked foil book-marker can be given at the same time.

The right-hand book jacket shown on page 28, top left, is made from gold foil.

The photograph album in the same picture is covered in silver foil on which the bust and title are worked and emphasized in black as described on page 24. The rest of the jacket is worked with a tracing-wheel and then painted blue.

CIGARETTE-BOX
For the container you can use any holder of suitable size and shape. Line it inside and out with green crepe-paper (or foil, as shown in the illustration on page 26, top). The brass foil is marked out as shown in fig. 4 on page 27, the individual scallops being de-lineated with a pair of dividers and then cut to the end of the unbroken line shown in the diagram. Each scallop is impressed with dots or stars as shown, and the box is supplied with a monogram (if you want one) and a pattern. Further lustre is added to the mono-gram by painting it in transparent yellow. Finally, the cover is glued to the container and the scallops are folded outwards.

TOBACCO-BOX
If a friend of yours smokes a pipe, why not give him a decorated tobacco-box? Any suitably sized container will do. The box shown on page 28, top right, was given two coats of dark-blue poster paint. After having been set to dry, it was rubbed with clear wax and then brought to a final brilliance

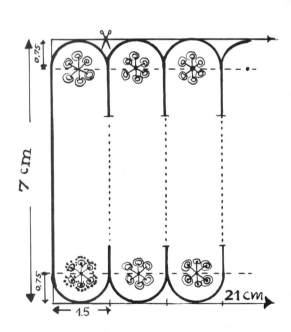

Fig. 4

with a brush and a soft cloth. On the side, the word 'Tobacco' was fixed with adhesive after the individual letters had been cut out and patterned. The illustration shows a flame-rosette on the lid of the box (see fig. 5, page 29). After cutting out from the foil, the individual rays are strongly embossed before fixing with adhesive.

In winter, when fresh flowers are so expensive, a foil bouquet makes a welcome and lasting gift. We can get many ideas from the arrangements of artificial flowers to be seen in the flower shops. Foil flowers can be fixed with pins on Styrofoam balls or pyramids, or they can be used to make attractive wreaths. Small bouquets can be used to decorate gift packages. Attractive wall-hangings can be made by fixing foil flowers and leaves in a webbing band or sticking them into a thick plait of natural or dark-green raffia.

Since silver foil can be painted in a wide variety of bold and delicate colours, we are not hindered by the limited range of colour available.

TRINKET-BOX

In great-grandmother's day, the type of trinket-box illustrated on page 26, bottom, was very popular as a container for buttons, ribbons, jewelry and so on. The lids were usually decorated with a rich display of tiny flowers. We can make equally attractive trinket-boxes by decorating them with beads, sequins and foil, especially the gay foil-

CANDLE-HOLDER

(page 26, top)

For this attractive gift you will need silver and gold foil, a plastic cup, one needle about 6cm (2¼in) long, plaster, a candle, and Deka-Colour.

The rim of the cup is measured (with a tape-measure), and a gold metal-foil strip of that length and a width of about 6cm (2¼in) is cut and prepared, as in fig. 6a on page 29, so that the scallops begin halfway across the width of the strip. After impressing the pattern, the strip is fixed with adhesive inside the rim of the cup so that the scalloped edge opens outwards.

The cup is then filled with plaster of Paris in the middle of which the needle is set with the point protruding about 3cm (1⅛in). After the plaster has set, the cup is covered with coloured felt, velvet, paper or foil, or even painted in colour. The lower part of the cup is decorated, as shown in the illustration, with a foil strip cut and imprinted as in fig. 6b and then glued to the cup.

To cover the plaster-surface, a silver foil disc is cut out and impressed as in fig. 6c. The inner circle has the same diameter as the top of the cup, while the scalloped rays add 2 or 3cm (¾ or 1⅛in) to the diameter of the outer circle. A hole is punched in the middle of the disc which is then fitted over the needle and glued to the surface of the plaster. The scallops unfold upwards and outwards and serve to catch the candle-grease as well as to decorate the holder.

The effect is improved by coating the candle with a transparent metallic colour to match the colour of the cup. Cotton-wool dipped in candle-dye is used, and after drying (which may take some time), you can, if you want, add a personal touch by cutting your friend's name into the candle.

FLOWERS

Foil flowers are not only attractive but easy to make. The basic shape is circular. The circle is drawn with a pair of dividers which, set to the same radius, is used to mark off six arcs around the circumference. These establish the mid-point of the petals along the circumference. Six (or even twelve) petals may then be shaped and cut, as in fig. 8 on page 29, before impressing with lines or dots. They will then unfold of themselves into petals.

A single blossom is made of two to four such discs in different sizes. They are pierced through the centre with a needle before fixing on wire or thread with Bostik No. 1. The blossom is topped with a glass-bead or tin-foil ball.

To make a foil-bouquet the single blossoms are fixed on green floristry wire which is bent at the top (preferably with pliers) and stuck into the tin-foil ball. If instead of fixing the discs of the blossoms with adhesive as shown, they are sewn together with thread, then a small glass bead is drawn with thread through a large bead fitted at the centre of the blossom which is then held together by knotting a sequin under the bottom disc.

If many flowers are to be made, the foil can be folded over a couple of times so that four discs can be cut out at the same time.

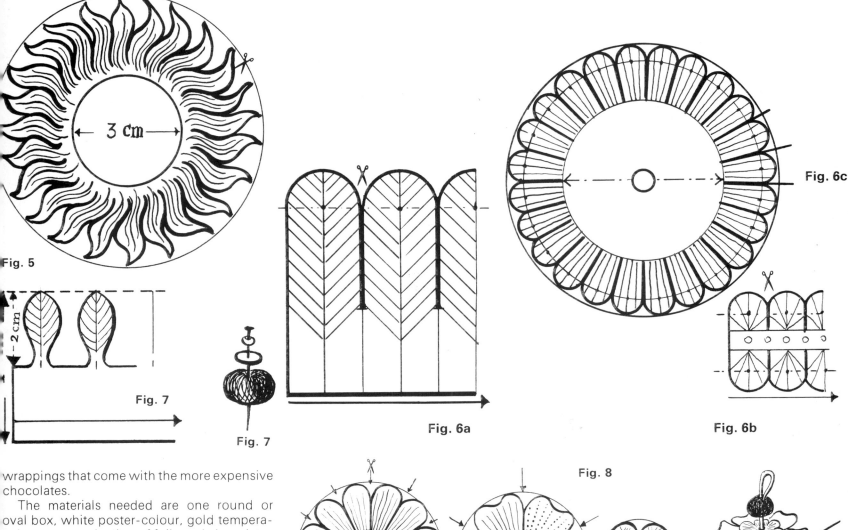

Fig. 5

Fig. 7

Fig. 7

Fig. 6a

Fig. 6b

Fig. 6c

Fig. 8

wrappings that come with the more expensive chocolates.

The materials needed are one round or oval box, white poster-colour, gold tempera-colour, a gay selection of foils and chocolate-wrappings, small sequins, beads (especially very small ones) white edging or braid, and for the inside lining, pink foil, gold paper, velvet or felt.

The first step is to give the outside of the box two coats of white, allow to dry and polish with soft rag or cotton wool. Given an airtight lining of foil or laminated paper, the box could be used to hold confectionery. A felt or velvet lining makes it suitable for trinkets only. To ensure a tight fit, the inside of the rim is painted.

The branches are cut from felt, and the pieces then carefully glued to the lid. A symmetrical framework of branches is made by folding the felt in two before cutting out one half of the pattern only. The individual flowers are cut and glued, both flat and in open relief, as illustrated, first sewing a tiny bead in the middle. Small branches and dots can be painted in gold, while gold sequins are used for the grapes.

The vase is worked in thick gold foil. The pattern is made to stand out by impressing it from the reverse side. It is partly covered with grey chocolate-wrapping paper and worked over again in such a way that here and there the gold shines through. The gold foil scalloping and the handles of the bowl are fixed so that they stand out from the surface. Finally the edge of the lid is supplied with attractive braiding beneath which gold sequins are stuck at intervals (see illustration).

FOIL TREE BLOSSOM

The glittering tree shown on page 27, top left is an appropriately festive decoration for special occasions such as weddings or anniversaries. The blossoms are mainly silver foil, with others in gold. Leaves are green and tin-foil balls are violet. The colours can be varied to suit the occasion.

You need a Styrofoam ball 12–15cm (4¾–6in) diameter, a plastic flower-pot with a top diameter of 10–12cm (4–4¾in), foil for the blossoms, tin-foil for the balls, beads, sequins, pins, white velvet ribbon, plaster and white poster colour.

Fill the flower-pot with the plaster of Paris mixture, and while still soft, plant the stem in the middle and let the plaster dry. After the plaster has set, both the pot and the stem are painted white. Bore a hole in the Styrofoam ball so that later it can be fixed to the top of the stem. Then add the decorations.

The blossoms are made from foil discs (diameters 2, 3, and 4cm (¾, 1⅛, 1½in)) in the same way as the flowers described in fig. 8. Pins with small beads, sequins or tin-foil balls are stuck through the centre of the flowers and their layer of leaves. These complete flowers are then pinned all over the Styrofoam ball. It is not difficult to find appropriate fillers for any empty spaces there might be at the end.

The rim of the flower pot is decorated with a 4cm-wide (1½in) strip of green foil, cut in the pattern shown in fig. 7 so that the separate leaves fold inwards and can subsequently be glued onto the plaster surface. Tasselled braid is then fixed over the green-foil (as illustrated). If there is enough time, names and the details and date of the special occasion, can be painted in green on the white pot.

Finally, the decorated ball is fixed to the top of the stem (as shown) and the white velvet ribbon, with its bead-ends, is tied in an attractive bow just under the ball of blossoms.

Make sure that you start work early, if the

result is to be ready in time. If you want one of these colourful balls as a hanging decoration, then before decorating it, pierce it with a knitting-needle and draw a ribbon or nylon-thread through it.

FLOWER-GIRL *(page 27, top centre)*

The materials you will need are 2 lengths of floristry-wire, a paper- or wooden-ball of 2cm ($\frac{3}{4}$in) diameter, gold metal-foil for eight 9cm ($3\frac{1}{2}$in) long leaves, eight large beads, eight small beads (or eight sequins), black wool for the hair, silver and gold laminated paper (the layers of tin-foil are applied until the arms and torso have the right bulk).

A face is painted on the ball. The hair is then glued in place and decorated with a crown of blossoms as shown.

The skirt is made from a base of drawing paper, out of which cut a semi-circle (radius 9cm ($3\frac{1}{2}$in)) from drawing paper to form the cone shown in the illustration. Yellow paper (or crêpe-paper) is glued over the cone. The nine leaves are cut from gold foil, and veins are impressed.

Four or five of them may be painted with yellow Deka-Colour. The skirt-cone is then firmly fixed and glued to the torso and the join covered with a narrow ribbon after gluing the gold leaves to the bodice. The hem is decorated with flowers and beads. The head is fixed on the wire, and the neck is covered by a narrow ribbon-collar. The flower-girl carries a small tray of flowers.

CREPE-PAPER FLOWERS

These are shown on page 27, right. The heart of the flower consists of a tin-foil ball stuck on floristry-wire. One method is to make a flower by gluing a number of sufficiently large blossom-discs (as illustrated in fig. 8) around the ball. Another is to fold a long strip of crêpe-paper and to wrap it around the ball, with the fold upwards, until one has the kind of firm blossom illustrated in the bottom right-hand corner of the picture.

CANDLE-LADY

Figure 9 on page 32 shows the first steps in making the attractive gift shown in the picture on page 27, right. You will need a white ball of 4–5cm ($1\frac{1}{2}$–2in) diameter, a bottle-cork, black wool for the hair, a knitting needle, a 30cm ($11\frac{4}{5}$in) length of wire, gold and silver laminated paper, coloured tin-foil, crimson crêpe-paper, blue ribbon, two small candles about 8cm ($3\frac{1}{8}$in) long and 1cm ($\frac{1}{3}$in) thick, white poster paint, and an empty bottle or container about 18–20cm (7–7$\frac{3}{4}$in) high.

After trimming the cork to taper somewhat towards the top, the needle, cork, wire and ball are fixed together as shown in the diagram. Paint the face and neck. The torso is formed with cotton-wool covered in ordinary tin-foil, over which a final layer of coloured

in-foil is glued to make the dress. The hair is glued on, the decorations are fixed in place as illustrated, and then the finished torso is set in a bottle or container filled with sand for stability. This base is covered with crêpe-paper and further decorated with blue ribbon. The torso can also be decorated with a narrow, patterned braid as shown. The candles in their cups of blue foil are fixed as shown in the diagram. The crêpe-paper flowers lend an elegant touch to it all.

MIRROR

The illustration on page 31, top, shows the effectiveness of mounting a mirror inside the round lid of a paint-tin or similar container and decorating it in colours that will harmonize with the room for which it is intended.

The materials needed are a lid of about 23cm (9in) diameter, a round mirror with a diameter of 19cm (7½in), velvet-cord, gold metal-foil for the 13 blossoms, 13 beads, 1 brass curtain-ring, pins, Bostik No. 1 for fixing the glass, cardboard ring, with an inner diameter of 18·5cm (7¼in) and a width of 1·5cm (⅗in).

A strip of velvet-cord 75cm (29½in) long and 14cm (5½in) wide is cut out and glued around the lid. The mirror is then glued exactly in the middle of the underside of the lid. The cardboard ring is also covered with a 3cm (1⅛in) strip of velvet-cord before gluing over the mirror so that its outer rim is concealed.

Twelve flowers (4cm (1½in) diameter) are made from gold and stuck with a pin and

bead in the raised outer frame of the mirror. The mirror is hung by means of a piece of doubled needle-cord measuring about 44cm (17$\frac{1}{3}$in) by 2 or 3cm ($\frac{3}{4}$ or 1$\frac{1}{8}$in), with a brass ring sewn at the top and both ends joined together and sewn or glued to the back.

A gold foil blossom adds to the decorative effect by being attached just below the brass ring. Finally, the back of the mirror is neatly covered with velvet or felt.

FLAT MIRROR

This has a diameter of 19cm (7$\frac{1}{2}$in) (size is not important). It should be decorated in such a way that it matches the wall that it hangs on.

In addition to the mirror, one will need two thin cardboard discs, some velvet-cord, silver-foil or Alu-Foil and Bostik No. 1.

With an outer diameter of 30cm (11$\frac{4}{5}$in) and an inner diameter of 18cm (7in), a cardboard ring is cut and covered with velvet-cord which is glued on the back. The mirror is carefully glued on the back of the ring and left to dry under pressure.

A second ring, with an outer diameter of 29.8cm (11$\frac{3}{4}$in) and an inner diameter of 19.2cm (7$\frac{1}{2}$in), is glued to the back of the mirror so that it will have a flat surface.

A velvet-cord hanger is made, as shown in fig. 10a, from a strip measuring about 25cm (9$\frac{7}{8}$in) long and 7cm (2$\frac{3}{4}$in) wide, and folded and sewn to give a finished width of about 3cm (1$\frac{1}{8}$in). If you have no silver curtain-ring, you can use a cardboard ring cut to outer and inner diameters of 6 and 3cm (2$\frac{1}{4}$ and 1$\frac{1}{8}$in) respectively and covered with silver foil, impressed as shown. The hanger is finally sewn or glued to the back of the mirror.

The border decoration is made from a strip of foil about 4cm (1$\frac{1}{2}$in) wide and 80cm (31$\frac{1}{2}$in) long, which is marked and cut as shown in fig. 10b. (This border can be made with two, or even four, shorter foil strips, of course.)

Having impressed a design as shown, you can use pins (as in fig. 10c) to place the border tentatively in position, bearing in mind that raising the connecting strip between the leaves and flowers (by means of a brush as shown in fig. 10c) not only enhances the appearance but also gives some flexibility in arranging the decorative border correctly, before finally fixing it with pins.

For calculating the length of foil-strip needed for mirrors of other sizes, you multiply the diameter by 3·145 and add one-third of the result to allow for the 'humps' shown in the diagram. It is possible, but more difficult, to cut the decorative border out of a sheet of foil so that you get a ring with a 21cm (8$\frac{1}{4}$in) inner and a 29cm (11$\frac{2}{5}$in) outer diameter.

By pinning only the narrow connecting band and leaving the leaves and flowers free, you can at any time take off this decoration and replace with a new one.

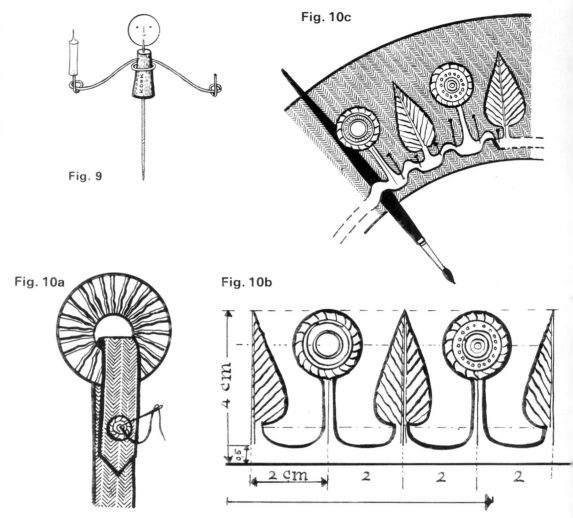

Fig. 9

Fig. 10a   Fig. 10b

Fig. 10c

GARDEN OF EDEN SCENE
(page 30, top)

This is an example of using exotic chocolate-wrappings to the best advantage while keeping their crinkly appearance to enhance the effect even further. A black-painted cardboard background is used for mounting the foils.

These are best handled with tweezers. Coat them with adhesive and fix them firmly in position. The name and the date below the picture, but also such things as the branches and dot-patterns, can be done in gold poster paint.

The picture is best set off in an old gold frame, but the glass can equally well be held in position with a black passe-partout strip about 1·5cm ($\frac{3}{4}$in) wide which is then decorated with narrow strips of gold foil impressed with dots at intervals and fixed with adhesive.

OVAL FLOWER-PICTURE *(page 30)*

The illustration shows how an old frame can be used to enclose an attractive bouquet of flowers made up of a combination of artificial flowers and leaves made from foil, set against a wine-red damask background.

HEAD-BAND AND DECORATION

These are to be regarded more as ideas for fancy-dress and theatre costumes than as presents and gifts.

The picture on page 33, top shows how an Egyptian-style head decoration may be made from a head band, five to ten metres of satin cord, and green and gold metal-foil.

The green foil is cut into a number of semi-circles with a radius of 1·25 or 1·5cm (about $\frac{3}{5}$in). They are then formed into cones from which the tip is cut off. The cord is cut into 35cm (13$\frac{3}{4}$in) lengths, and as well as knots at each end, other knots are sewn in with thick yarn at 4cm (1$\frac{1}{2}$in) intervals on the cord. The foil cones are folded over the knots and glued into position. The finished cords are then sewn to the headband. You can decide for yourself what length cord and how many decorative cones you will have.

The head-band is decorated with the gold foil discs. They will have a diameter of about 5cm (2in), and any pattern that takes your fancy. The pointed strip fixed to the back of the disc (fig. 11) is used to hold it in position (by folding it over the head-band). The finishing touch is given by sewing a glass or tin-foil bead to the centre of each disc.

HIGH FASHION WIG
(page 31, bottom right)

This is a brilliant, eye-catching creation to be worn in a play, with fancy-dress costume or evening-dress, and one likely to take pride of place in a shop-window display.

To make it you will need a made-up or

discarded helmet-type hat as the base, a hat-shop display head, crêpe-paper, and gold and silver aluminium foil. The colours of the crêpe-paper flowers should suit the dress with which the wig will be worn, and rather than a riot of colour, they should be just the light and dark tones of the same colour.

Silver and gold aluminium-foil strips (about 1·5cm ($\frac{3}{5}$in) wide and 10 to 16cm (4–6$\frac{1}{4}$in) long) are used to make the ringlets by winding them into spirals on a pencil. The base should be thickly covered with the curls, which are sewn on, and with the flowers of crêpe-paper. Make stars to add even more glitter to the wig. The final touch of elegance is given by the beads added to the front of the wig, as shown in the illustration.

PIN-CUSHION LADY AND SEWING STAND

The picture, bottom left on page 31 illustrates the charming way in which we can have our sewing materials both attractively displayed and close to hand.

Figure 12 shows what materials are needed: a Styrofoam ball of 7cm diameter, a plastic container about 9 or 10cm (3$\frac{1}{2}$–4in) high, felt, wool or acrylic yarn for the hair, one 10cm (4in) long needle, short gold pins, sequins, foil and plaster.

The empty plastic container is filled with plaster of Paris. The needle is inserted in it while still soft so that about 7·5cm (2$\frac{7}{8}$in)

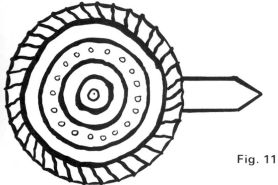

Fig. 11

protrudes as shown. The bottle is then coated with adhesive before covering with felt. The base is made as illustrated in the diagram with two felt discs (diameter about 14·5cm (5$\frac{3}{4}$in)), between which is glued a cardboard disc with a diameter 2cm ($\frac{3}{4}$in) larger than that of the bottom of the bottle. The two felt discs are sewn together at the edge. A small strip of material the same colour as the hair can look very pretty if sewn between the edges of the two felt discs (see illustration, page 31). The base is glued to the bottom of the bottle, and arranged, as shown in the picture. Their positions properly arranged, the pockets are firmly fixed by means of gold pins pushed through small sequins. Each separate pocket can be decorated with a gold foil blossom and bead centre as shown.

To make the head, the Styrofoam ball is painted white and allowed to dry. Coloured pins are stuck through blue sequins to make the eyes. The mouth and cheeks can be done in pink either with a felt-tipped pen or with transparent red paint (if the first attempt fails, then white poster paint can be used to cover up before a further attempt is made).

For the hair, pieces of wool about 20cm (7$\frac{3}{4}$in) long are glued with Copydex adhesive to the top of the head as shown in fig. 12, and two long plaits are made as shown in the illustration on page 31.

The ruffled collar is made from a felt disc about 9cm (3$\frac{1}{2}$in) in diameter, its edge shaped as shown in the diagram. Small white buttons are sewn to the edge, as in the picture on page 31. A hole is made in the middle so that it fits over the knitting needle. Another felt disc covers the plaster in the bottle.

After fitting everything together as shown in the diagram, a waist-band is made out of the same material as the hair, and arranged, as shown in the diagram, to take a small pair of scissors. The sling around the scissors can be decorated with sequins and small beads.

PIN-CUSHION LADY

Page 31, top, shows another handy ornament which can be made with an egg-cup shaped cosmetic-jar, a Styrofoam ball corresponding in diameter to that of the top of the jar-lid, braid or lace, a cardboard cylinder about 4cm (1$\frac{1}{2}$in) tall and of the same diameter as the base of the jar, and a needle about 7cm (2$\frac{3}{4}$in) long.

The lid of the jar is removed and a hole is bored in the middle. The ball is sawn with a fret-saw and one of the halves is bored through the middle. The ball and lid are glued together with Copydex adhesive and the needle is pushed through the hole to protrude about 2cm ($\frac{3}{4}$in) at the top.

Beginning at the point of the needle, the head is tied around with thick wool which is fixed into position with Copydex. A woollen plait is woven and glued around the lid as shown in fig. 13.

Using Deka-Colours, a pretty face is then

Fig. 12

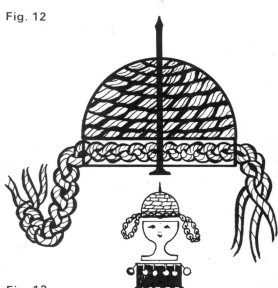

Fig. 13

painted on the cup of the cosmetic-jar. Nail-polish is excellent for the lips.

The pedestal is made from a cardboard cylinder as used for holding dairy-cream or winding woollen-yarn. Its diameter should correspond to that of the cosmetic-jar. It is covered with cloth, felt, velvet or foil, before being glued to the jar (as shown in the diagram and picture). The join is hidden with a strip of trimming or lace. The base is decorated with a plait made from the same material as the hair. The protruding needle-point is covered with chocolate-wrapping and finally topped with a thimble or cotton reel.

Since the pin-cushion head can be unscrewed, the cup of the jar can be used to hold buttons and other small items.

Soft Toys

INTRODUCTION

As each toy in this chapter has been designed by a different toymaker you will notice that an interesting variety of toymaking methods have been used. Some of these toys were intended for older children or for more decorative purposes. If you wish to make them for young children certain modifications will be necessary for perfect safety. For example, the hair on the lovely Japanese Puppet could be made from wool instead of small beads, and spots of coloured felt could replace the sequins on the Clown. Eyes should be embroidered for very young children.

Although this book is aimed at those who already have some experience in toymaking, a careful beginner should be able to produce a worthwhile result by paying particular attention to the following sections.

These are general instructions only. Where a different method of approach is used this is explained in the individual instructions.

Enlarging the Patterns

Take a piece of plain paper, large enough to accommodate the full size pattern. Mark out in squares (the scale of the toys varies—the correct size is marked on each diagram). Now copy the patterns, square by square, from the diagrams supplied and add all pattern markings. Accuracy at this stage is most important

if a well fitting toy is to be the result.

If the patterns are to be used more than once, either draw them straight on to thin card or paste the enlarged pattern on to card and cut round the outlines. It is a good idea to keep each pattern in a large envelope, clearly marked with the name or a drawing of the toy, and the number of pattern pieces.

Cutting Out

Make sure all pattern markings have been transferred to enlarged pattern pieces. The arrows indicate the direction of the grain of the fabric or 'stroke' of the pile. Broken lines mark fold of fabric in some cases, turnings or cutting line (Cub) in others. Dotted lines refer to positions of features, openings for stuffing or quilting lines (Dragon).

Lay pattern pieces on the wrong side of chosen material. Check that the selvedge edge runs in the same direction as arrows marked on patterns (or that pile strokes in direction of arrows). Make sure that you space pattern pieces to allow for turnings (unless already allowed), and the number of pieces which are marked on pattern shapes (cut extra shapes if you are uncertain).

When using materials with a right and wrong side, such as fur fabric, remember to reverse the pattern where the shape is an assymetrical one (e.g. body of Cub). Pin the paper patterns to the fabric, or hold the card patterns on fabric with a heavy weight. Draw thin, clean lines round patterns using tailor's chalk on dark fabrics, pencil on light ones. Cut out carefully, using very sharp scissors.

Sewing Up

The following are general instructions. Specific stitches are given with individual instructions.

1. It is helpful to use contrasting threads to mark positions of ears, limbs and portions to be left open for stuffing.

2. Tack sections together first, then back-stitch with small, firm stitches. Portions such as the Clown's body and limbs and many parts of the Dragon can be successfully machine stitched, but generally more control will be achieved by hand sewing.

3. Keep turnings even throughout and match letters marked on patterns and portions to be left open for stuffing.

4. Use ladder stitch (diagram page 37) for closing seams on the right side and for joining on separate sections—e.g. Clown's limbs, Cub's nose, tail. When the stitches are pulled up tightly, the raw edges are turned to the inside and the stitches rendered invisible.

Stuffing

Choose a stuffing appropriate to the toy—e.g. foam chips wash and dry well, kapok is light and moulds well, shredded waste is economical.

Stuffing determines the final shape of the toy. Aim to preserve details of pattern and obtain a smooth, even surface on each section as you go along. Work slowly and carefully using small quantities of stuffing, filling the toy too hard rather than too soft. Remember that if a section is badly stuffed it can only be improved by taking out the stuffing and starting again.

Always stuff the extremities first, using a stuffing stitch, knitting needle or pencil to help you. Ladder stitch openings together when stuffing is completed.

EMBROIDERED BALL (picture and diagrams, page 36. Colour picture, this page)

The decorative theme of 'everyday animals' used for this ball was inspired by drawings from children's books and birthday cards. You can copy our theme or choose one of your own.

Designer's comment: 'I tried to create a simple ball which would satisfy its small owner's eyes and brain—as well as his hands, feet and teeth!'

Materials

Pentagons: 11 × 14in turquoise felt
Triangles: 8 × 5in yellow felt; 5 × 4in dark blue felt; 5 × 4in cerise felt
Stranded cotton embroidery threads
Sewing threads to match felt
Small pieces of felt, assorted colours
Chips of foam rubber or Terylene wadding for stuffing

To make

Patchwork pieces Trace off the Triangle and Pentagon and transfer to thin card. Cut out accurately. Use templates to cut 12 pentagons, 10 yellow triangles, 5 blue triangles and 5 cerise triangles in felt.

Each shape must be accurate or it will be difficult to assemble the shapes attractively.

Decoration Cut chosen shapes from thin card (one to fit inside each pentagon). Cut each main shape in felt (i.e. basic body shape if using animals). Sew a shape to each pentagon with fancy stitching. Embroider details such as features, tails, petals, with as much variety in colour and stitchery as possible. Keep any background scenery suitable to the subject and use only one strand of embroidery thread so that it does not detract from the subject.

Take great care not to stretch or pucker the pentagons.

To assemble

Oversew pieces following diagram (keeping the chosen decorations all the same way up), to form two half sections.

The curve X Y Z forms the 'equator' of the ball. Sew halves together, leaving an opening for stuffing. Stuff to give a firm, round shape. If foam rubber is used the ball will be more bouncy. Oversew opening to finish.

TIPO BUFFO (pattern and diagram, page 37. Colour picture, page 38)

At around three feet eight inches high our lovable Clown is likely to be larger than his owner! Tipo Buffo means 'Funny Fella' in Italian and his splendidly bendable arms, legs and fingers make sure he will live up to his name.

Designer's comment: 'I am a compulsive doodler, and one day, from a doodle, Tipo Buffo emerged'.

Materials

Face and Toe: 24 × 12in flesh coloured felt
Body, Legs, Arms: ½yd calico, 36in wide
Tunic: 1yd bonded (or fairly stiff) material 60in wide (or 1¾yd of 36in fabric)
Boots: 18in square black felt of 'wet look' plastic; pair child's shoe laces o 1½yd white ribbon, ½in wide; piece thin card, 8in square
Gloves: Pair child's knitted white cotton gloves or 18in square of white felt
Frills: 2 strips blue, 2 strips green nylon net, each 9 × 36in
Small packet mixed sequins
Hair: 1oz orange 'Fun Fur' yarn or very thick knitting yarn
Features: 9in square white felt; 9in square red felt; scraps felt in black, royal blue; 2 'goggle' eyes, ¾in diameter
Sundries:
12in wooden dowel about ½in thick
44 and 50in lengths thick wire
10 pipecleaners
1½lb Dacron or Terylene wadding or kapok
Linen thread: Terylene machine thread
White fabric adhesive
Reel of sticking plaster

To make

Trace off features from enlarged pattern of head and cut out in felt (use colour photo as

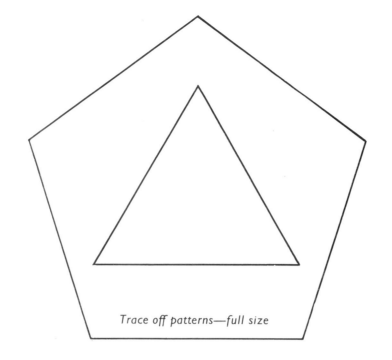

Trace off patterns—full size

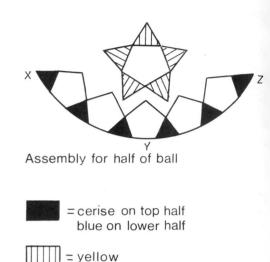

Assembly for half of ball

█ = cerise on top half
blue on lower half

▥ = yellow

a guide, but cut 3 red face spots). Enlarge and cut out other pattern pieces—see page 34. Make up each section separately, then assemble.

Turnings of $\frac{1}{4}$in are allowed.

Clip all curved seams before turning.

Head Sew darts. Sew round head leaving A–A open. Turn and stuff. To make ears, ease stuffing back between OO–OO. Stab stitch as indicated on pattern.

Toe Leaving X–X open, stitch and turn. Stuff. Cut flesh nail, white detail and glue parts of nail in position.

Boots (makes 2 alike) Glue card sole to fabric sole. Stab stitch sole A–B to upper A–B at each side. Stitch back seam B–E of upper. Stitch front from A to cross below lacing holes. Stitch felt toe to one boot between X and X. Stuff toes of boots.

Gloves Stab stitch felt gloves together in pairs or use bought ones. Stuff fingers at ends only. Take each pipecleaner and bend ends back for $\frac{1}{4}$in. Bind ends with plaster. Push a pipecleaner up each finger (see pattern) and stuff to hold it in place. Stuff palms.

Prepare body wires With pliers, turn over 2in at ends and bind well with plaster to secure wire and pad ends. Wrap entire length of wires with strips of rag, stitching to hold firmly in place.

Dowel Wrap in rags and stitch as for wires.

Tunic Stitch upper arms (H–I). Stitch sides (F–G). Slash each piece from K to J, then stitch front to back from K–J and down J–K of other leg. Press and turn.

Legs Stitch in pairs leaving ends D–D open. Turn and stuff base of each leg.

Arms Make up as for legs. Take 44in wire, push an end down one arm. With stick, pad well all round wire. Insert other end of wire into other arm, repeat stuffing. (Straight centre of wire fits over shoulders.)

Take 50in wire and repeat for legs.

Bend arm and leg wires as shown in wiring diagram.

Body Stitch from B1 to D at each side. Leave D–D and B1–A open. Turn.

Body Assembly Stuff base of body. Insert curved part of leg wire into body base, stitch back to front at D1. Stuffing as you go, ladder stitch each leg D–D to D–D1 of body. Insert legs of body into legs of tunic and pull tunic up body. Turn in raw edges of tunic legs. Stitch to legs matching E–E.

Insert ends of arms into sleeves. Lay centre arm wire across body from B to B. Stitch A–B each side leaving neck open. Stuff remainder of body firmly and ladder stitch arms to body (B–B1).

Insert half the dowel into body at neck, keeping arm wire to back. Stitch rags on wire and dowel firmly together. Stuff neck and shoulders well. Insert top of dowel into head (still stuffing as you go). Bring neck of head over body neck and stitch.

It is important to stuff neck firmly. Using a long needle and linen thread, pass the needle through from back to front several times, then side to side, catching in dowel rags as you do so.

Stitch tunic 1–A1 both sides. Draw up neck edge, turn in raw edge and ladder stitch to base of neck. Ladder stitch gloves to ends of arms. Ladder stitch tunic sleeves to glove cuffs. Push legs into boots, make holes for laces or ribbon and thread these in, then tie in a bow on each boot. Ladder stitch boot tops to legs.

Face Gather round edge of nose. Stuff, draw up tightly and stitch to head. Stick other features in place as on pattern.

Hair With matching thread, stitch on double row of yarn loops along top head join from ear to ear.

Frills Lay rectangles of net on top of each other, alternating colours. Gather along centre, draw up to fit neck and stitch in place. Sew or stick on sequins. Add two or three black bobbles or felt circles to tunic front to finish.

CUDDLY CUB (pattern and diagrams, pages 38, 39 and 40. Colour picture, page 39)

This delightful design would make an appealing toy or mascot—or with slight adaptations—a friendly pyjama case.

Designer's comment: 'I bought the fur fabric first. This gave me the idea for a Cub. I had used his head idea before to make a bear.'

Materials

18 × 33in Ocelot Acrilan fur fabric (body, ears, head gusset, head, tail).

20 × 32in long pile white fur fabric (underbody, ear lining, lower side of face, top of foot, inside legs).

12in square short pile white fur fabric (nose top, bottom mouth, eye patch).

12 × 3in black or brown short pile fur fabric (ear piping).

6in square green (eye (medium)), black (eye (large and small))) and flesh felt should be used for tongue, roof of mouth, lower inside mouth.

10in square (or 18 × 5in strip) of brown leather, felt or soft synthetic leather (pads).

White stranded cotton.

Black and white button thread.

Nylon (invisible) thread for whiskers.

Black or brown pencils.

Fabric adhesive.

Sewing threads to match fabrics.

Large, strong needle (for hand sewing).

Nylon or Terylene stuffing (about $1\frac{1}{4}$lb).

To make

Enlarge and cut out pattern pieces (remembering to reverse assymetrical shapes—see page 34). When cutting pile fabric snip through backing only, not through pile.

Turnings of $\frac{3}{16}$ in are allowed.

Body and legs Join body from A to B. Join each white (inside) Front and Back Leg to body between broken line and Q.

Feet Sew on Tops of Feet, matching E—Q—E, and gathering to fit as necessary.

Sew on Pads, matching D, E, R, E, and gathering to fit. Close each leg seam from broken line to D. Turn to right side. Stuff feet fairly firmly. Using strong black thread stitch dividing lines for toes as in diagram.

Ears Sew piping to each Ocelot Ear with small running stitches and gather to fit ear lining. Tack and then sew all three sections together along stitching line for piping. Turn to right side and slightly gather along lower edge of inner ears.

Nose Top and Mouth Fold Nose Top in half, right sides together, and stitch from fold to K. Fold as shown in the second diagram, and stitch $\frac{1}{2}$ in down. Cut off point above stitching.

Pin nose top to Roof of Mouth, matching points X and L. Gather to fit and then stitch on wrong side.

Sew fur fabric Bottom Mouth to felt Lower Inside Mouth, gathering to fit as necessary. Turn right side out and pinch felt up into a lip all round sewn edge. Top stitch over previous line of stitching to secure (third diagram). Sandwich Tongue between lower inside mouth and roof of mouth. Stitch sections together through three layers of felt only.

Head assembly Pin Lower Side of Face to nose and mouth sections, matching points H and N. Sew in place, gathering to fit.

Pin Ocelot Head to white Eye Patch, matching points F and G. Stitch.

Sew darts in Head Gusset. Sew head gusset to head matching points H, J, P and O.

Features *Nose:* Run a gather thread round edge of nose. Stuff firmly, draw up gather thread tightly and fasten off. Shape nostrils with stab stitches (fourth diagram), and ladder stitch nose to head.

Eyes: Glue layers of felt together for each eye (black, green, black) with fabric adhesive and glue to furry eye patches. When dry, stitch a white highlight through centre of each eye with stranded cotton.

Markings Using black or brown pencil, dipped in water, shade in beneath eyes. Mark dots on either side of nose top section for positions of whiskers.

Whiskers Using double 'invisible' thread, sew sets of whiskers, 3 to 4in long, through marked dots (diagram page 39).

Ears Sew on where marked, using ladder stitch.

Head finish Run a gather thread along lower raw edges and draw up loosely. Stuff fairly firmly, stab stitching in final shaping as shown in diagram, page 39.

Body finish Close front seam between tops of legs and O. Stitch tuck in Underbody. Sew underbody to body, matching points C and O. Stitch as far as possible on the

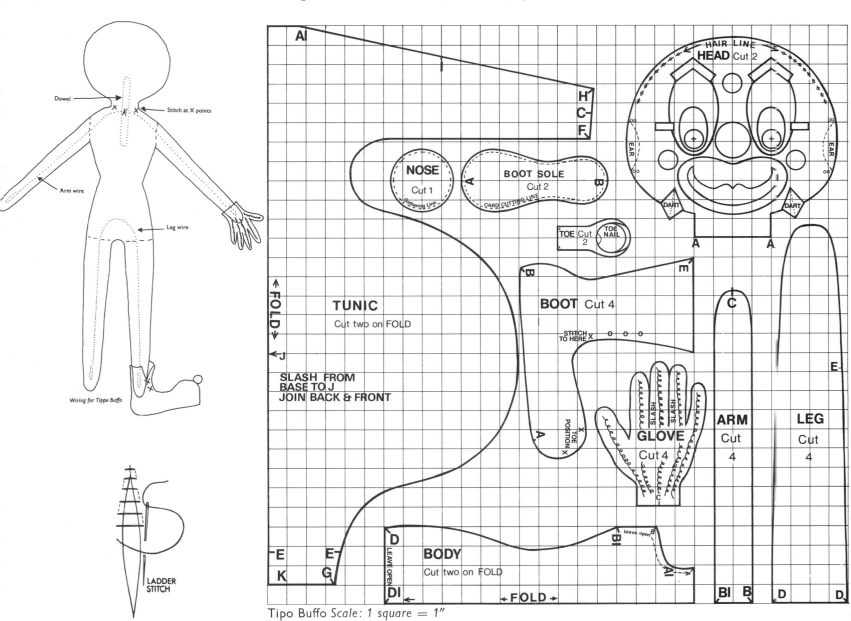

Tipo Buffo Scale: 1 square = 1"

37

allowance is shown on pattern.

Head Cut a hole in Ball to receive Neck Tube, ensuring a tight fit. Take the four Foam Segments, cut a $4\frac{3}{4} \times 3\frac{1}{4}$in oblong of foam and use these pieces to cover ball and tube. Foam should be a snug fit. Adjust if necessary.

Now cover head and neck with silk, keeping fabric taut. To do this, join AA and BB at both sides on Face Section. Slash from O to C at neck end of Back of Head and face sections. Turn face section to right side and fit over head. Sew face and back of head together, turning under raw edges of face section and hemming over head section. Leave neck ends free and ensure a smooth taut surface. Cover neck with an oblong of silk and insert into head. Neaten raw neck edges on head section.

Hair Sew one Side to top of Hair Foundation matching EE and FF. Repeat at other side. With seams inside, stitch hair foundation to head, covering the face seams. Cover felt foundation with rows of beads as follows. Secure black thread at front edge of hair

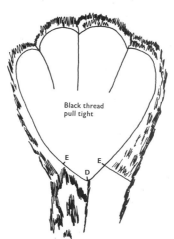

Fig. 1 Stitching detail on pad

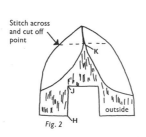

Fig. 2

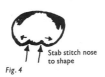

Fig. 4

inside, then turn to right side, leaving neck end open for stuffing.

Tail Neaten raw straight edge of Tail End and sew to end of Tail. Fold tail in half, right sides together and sew all round, leaving BC open for stuffing. Stuff firmly and ladder stitch to body.

To finish

Stuff body firmly and ladder stitch head in place, adding more stuffing if necessary. Stroke all seams carefully with a pin to free sewn-in pile. Give a final grooming with a brush and comb.

MING-SOO THE JAPANESE PUPPET

(patterns and diagrams on page 41)
This charming hand puppet will provide hours of enjoyment. It is simple to make and with very few changes several companions could be made for a puppet play.

Designer's comment: 'The Puppet was prepared as an illustration of an interesting use of material oddments in the technique of applied and detached patch-work'.

Materials

Head Featherweight plastic or foam ball, $2\frac{1}{2}$in diameter
10in square of plastic foam, $\frac{1}{4}$in thick
Stiff cardboard tube, $1\frac{1}{8}$in diameter, $3\frac{1}{2}$in long (for neck)
9×36in light brown silk (face, neck, hands)
12in square black felt (hair foundation)
150 black bugle beads and 150 black beads (about 1mm)
Strong black thread
2 black 'star flower' sequins (eyes)
Dress $\frac{1}{4}$yd plain coloured poplin, 36in wide
$\frac{1}{4}$yd firm satin, 36in wide (lining)
$6 \times \frac{3}{4}$in and $6 \times \frac{1}{2}$in curtain rings (overdress)
Skein coton à broder (embroidery cotton) or 3 ply wool
24in square thin card (templates)
12 pieces silky dress material, small patterns (8×6in approximately)
$\frac{1}{2}$yd cream cotton lace, $\frac{1}{4}$in wide (cuff trim)

To make

Enlarge and cut out pattern pieces. Turning

foundation, $\frac{1}{2}$in up from bottom of felt. Pass thread through a bugle bead and a small black bead, then back through same bugle bead and into felt (top diagram).

Spacing beads $\frac{1}{4}$in apart, sew on rows of beads until entire hair foundation is covered.
Eyes Cut off lower half of sequins and stitch in place.
Mouth Embroider small 'O' shape in red thread.
Dress and hands Sew sides and shoulder seams of Dress, then Lining. Place lining inside dress, seams together. Tack hem and cuffs of dress and lining together and then bind with bias binding to match dress, cutting bias strips from left-over fabric. Trim cuffs with lace. Sew Hands together in pairs. Turn, insert a piece of foam in each, cut to hand shape. Insert hands in sleeve ends. Stitch cuffs together through wrist and end of hands as marked by dotted line on pattern. Place neck opening over neck of puppet. Turn in raw edge and hem in place.
Overdress Cut six Large Petal shapes from card. Cover with fabric, using different pattern back and front, and oversewing invisibly round the edges on the right side (a little fabric adhesive may help here).

Prepare six Small Petals in the same way, for collar. Use coton à broder (embroidery cotton) or oddments of 3 ply yarn to cover Curtain Rings in buttonhole stitch. Using

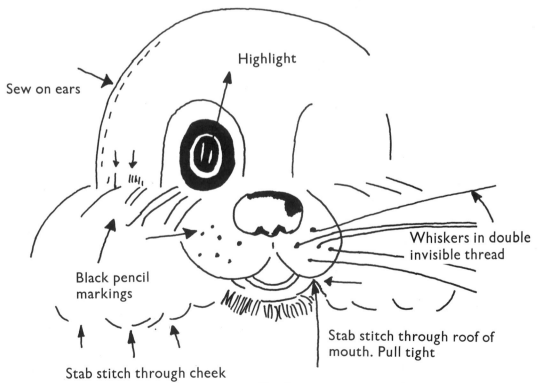

Fig. 5

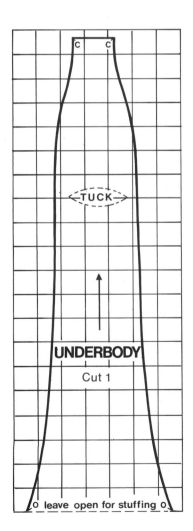

Within the pattern diagram:
TUCK
UNDERBODY
Cut 1
o leave open for stuffing o

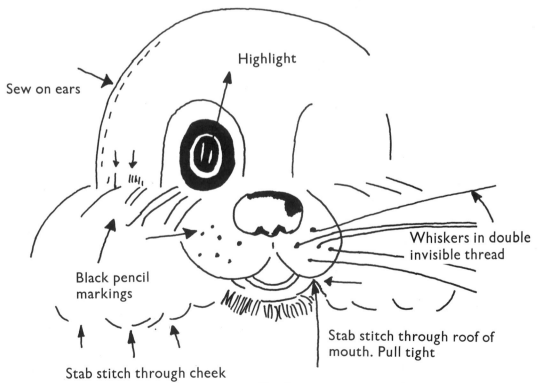

Within Fig. 5:
Sew on ears
Highlight
Whiskers in double invisible thread
Black pencil markings
Stab stitch through roof of mouth. Pull tight
Stab stitch through cheek

small rings at top and large rings at bottom, sew rings to large, covered petals as shown in lower diagram (work two halves at this stage). Sew small petals to top of large petals. Fit overdress on puppet and sew remaining sections. Cover twenty small petals on one side only and applique twelve round hem and four round each cuff.

PUFF THE BABY DRAGON

(patterns and diagrams on pages 43, 44, and 45. Colour picture page 34)
Complete in every detail—right down to his stuffed teeth—this magnificent dragon stands about two feet high and three feet long from nose to curled tail. In spite of his fierce expression Puff is really rather soft at heart!

Designer's comment: 'I like dragons— being mythical they offer more scope to the imagination than real animals. I have chosen here to make a friendly Baby Dragon'.

Materials

2yd of 36in wide light red felt
2¼yd of 36in wide medium red felt
¾yd of 36in wide dark red felt
12in square maroon felt
12 × 24in flesh or cream felt
12 × 18in white felt
Small piece black felt
1¼yd white or pink nylon lining, 36in wide
2yd cotton wadding, 18in wide
5lb kapok for stuffing
21ft of thick wire
2 × 2in flat button for eyes
5 pipecleaners
No. 60 sewing thread to match felts
Seam allowances are not shown on the pattern and must be added when cutting out. Allow ⅜in, trimming off surplus where necessary.

Much of the dragon is sewn by machine but there is also a great deal of hand-sewing. A curved surgical needle (obtainable at large chemists) will be found useful.

To make

Neck, Body and Tail Enlarge pattern (see page 34). Cut out the pattern pieces (adding turnings) for Neck, Body and Tail 1, 2 and 3 from Light Red Felt. Before sewing run a guide line in white cotton down the centre line of each piece, and where shown by the broken line. Mark small dotted lines with a different colour thread.

Sew the darts in each piece. Trim the wide darts. Machine neck to body, matching centre line and points A and B.

Machine body to Tail 1, matching centre line etc., and so on to the final tail piece.

Cut out Wadding for Neck, Body and Tail 1, 2 and 3. (Turnings are only necessary on the edges to be seamed.) Now cut a second piece of wadding for Neck, Body and Tail 1, trimming ½in off each side of these pieces. Cut Lining material ½in wider than the pattern for Body, Neck and Tail 1, 2 and 3. Machine lining pieces together, matching centre line and points A, C, E and G.

With wrong side of lining upwards place the narrow neck wadding on the neck lining, and the wider neck wadding on top of this, matching centre line. Tack through all three layers to hold wadding in place.

Follow the same method for body and first tail piece. Then tack the single layer of wadding in the rest of the tail.

With the felt wrong side upwards, place the lining on to the felt, sandwich the wadding between and match the centre line, points A, C, etc. Tack through all the layers to hold them firmly in place from neck to tail.

Starting at the top of the neck and on the right side of the felt, stitch across and through all the layers where shown by the dotted line. Continue until you reach the end of the tail. This gives the quilted effect.

Remove all tacking threads except for original guide lines. Cut off an 87in length of wire and bend it as nearly as you can to the shape in diagram, page 44, top left. The shaping need not be exact at this stage but make sure that point X, the bend at the base of the neck, is 32in from the front end of the wire. This wire runs from the tongue to the tail. Wire for the legs and arms will be joined on at a later stage.

Starting from point X on the wire and the felt, sew the centre back seam by hand from X to XX, sewing the wire securely into this seam. The seam will be covered so it need not be neat, but it must be strong.

At XX sew the back seam below the wire for 1in, then sew the wire into the seam for a further 5 or 6in. The wire for the legs will be joined on to the exposed inch of wire.

Temporarily close the base of the tail with several rows of tacking. Begin to fill the body with kapok, taking care not to strain the material where it is tacked together.

Return to point X and begin to sew the back neck seam, again leaving 1in of wire exposed and then incorporating the wire into the seam. The arms will be attached at X. Alternately sew and fill until you reach the top of the neck, making sure the stuffing is really firm and solid.

Cuddly Cub Scale: 1 square = 1"

Remove the temporary tacking from the base of the tail and fill the body firmly. To hold its shape the dragon must be solid. Sew the wire securely into the tail seam, again stopping every few inches to fill. Leave open the last 2in of tail.

Cut the Tail Arrow from Dark Red Felt. Sew together the two pieces from A through BCD to E, leaving the stem open. Trim and turn. Fill arrow with a little kapok, just to give it 'body'.

Turn in the edges of the stem and top-stitch as shown by the dotted line. Thread the arrow on to the end of the wire.

The tail should overlap the stem of the arrow at J by about $\frac{1}{4}$in. If necessary, trim the wire or the tail material.

Sew and fill the last inches of tail, this time keeping the wire inside. Neatly finish off the end of the tail at J.

Legs and Feet Take a 94in length of wire and thread it between the wire and the seam at XX. Wind round and through again as shown in right-hand diagram, leaving an equal length of wire each side of XX.

11in from XX bend the wire and shape for the foot as shown in the diagram. The back toe should be 3in long, each front toe 4in long.

Cut out the Feet and Toes in Medium Red Felt, and Toenails in Flesh or Cream Felt. Sew a toenail to each toe and ends of each foot along the curved line O to O. Trim seams.

Sew each toe to the corresponding toe on the foot, matching B to B and E to E. Trim and turn. Fill the first $\frac{1}{2}$in of each toe with kapok, then thread the wire into the toes. Fill firmly with kapok, ensuring that no wire can be felt through the material. Sew seams on top of the foot by hand, filling with kapok. Gather round leg-wire and fasten off firmly.

Cut the Outer and Inner Legs in light red felt and run a white cotton guide line where shown by broken line. Make the tucks Cut wadding and lining and quilt legs. Sew up the front seam AYB.

Trim the top edge of inner leg to the seam line and sew firmly to the body where shown

in diagram, page 44, top right, from M to N. Sew the wire very securely to the body for 9in from XX, sewing through the inner leg where necessary. Sew inner leg to body $\frac{1}{2}$in each side of wire.

Neatly sew the bottom of the leg to the foot, matching A to A and C to C. Sew up the back seam from C to N, filling the lower leg firmly as you go.

Trim the top curved edge of the upper leg to the seam line. Sew the last inch of the front seam to the body, then continue sewing the upper leg to the body until you reach the centre back.

Sew the last $\frac{1}{2}$in of the back leg seam to the body, Q to N, and continue to centre back, filling with kapok as you go. Keep the kapok firm in upper leg but thin it out towards the centre back seam. Sew the remaining top edge of the leg to the centre back seam, making sure all the wire is covered.

Cut the Leg Spurs from dark red felt, without seam allowance. Fold each spur and sew seam F to G neatly by hand. Fill firmly,

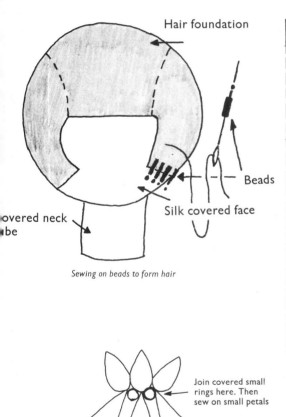

Sewing on beads to form hair

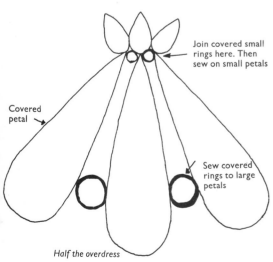

Half the overdress

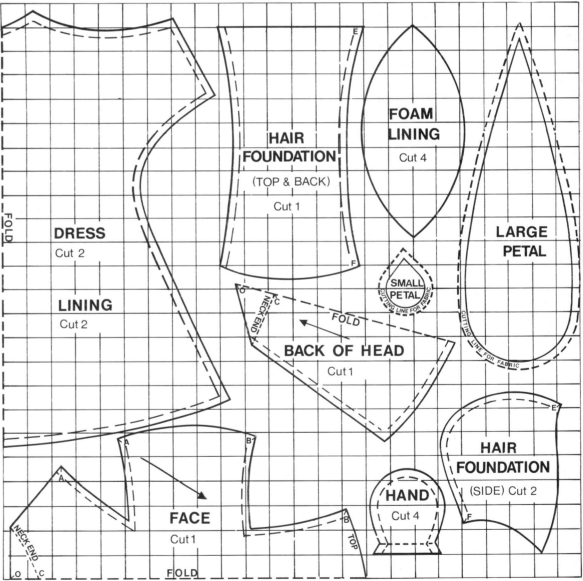

Ming-Soo the Japanese Puppet *Scale: 1 square = $\frac{1}{2}$"*

41

moulding the spur to the shape shown in the left-hand diagram. Sew securely to back of leg, below Q, as indicated on pattern.

Arms and Hands Take a 70in length of wire and join it to the back wire at X. Construct the skeleton for arms and hands exactly as you did for the legs and feet. The length of arm should be 8in, thumb 2in (corresponding to back toe), and fore fingers 3in.

Make up the hands and arms as you did the feet and legs, matching the points shown on the pattern.

Sew the top edge of the inner arm to the body. Sew the wire to the body 4in from X and sew the inner arm to the body $\frac{1}{4}$in each side of the wire.

Sew the bottom of the arm to the hand matching letters U and S. Sew up back seam and attach arm to body as for leg.

Make up the Spurs and sew onto arms where indicated on pattern.

Head Cut the Tongue from maroon felt. No seam allowance is needed. Top stitch the two pieces together as shown by the dotted line. Thread the wire into the tongue pushing in a little kapok first to blunt the end of the wire.

Cut the Teeth out of white felt. Sew the lower teeth together along the jagged edge. Trim and turn carefully. Fill each tooth with a little kapok and then stitch along the dotted line. Make the upper teeth in the same way.

Cut the Lips from medium red felt. Press the lower lip along fold line and stitch $\frac{3}{8}$in from the fold.

Join two pipecleaners by twisting the ends together and thread through the channel you have made. Bend back the two exposed ends to blunt them.

Tack the teeth to the lower lip, matching A, B, C and A. Sew through all thicknesses along the previous stitching line.

Make the upper lip, using two more pipe-cleaners, and attach to upper teeth in the same way.

Cut the Chin from light red felt. Quilt it and sew to the lower lip from A to A, matching B and C.

Cut the Nose and Back Head out of medium red felt. Press along the fold line J–J–J, stitch, and thread through the remaining pipecleaner. Quilt the nose.

Fold the two sides J into the middle J to form nostrils. Trim to the seam line and sew together J to K. Close inside of nostrils by sewing L to L.

Secure the end Js to centre J just behind the ridge formed by the pipecleaner.

Sew the nose to the upper lip, matching points P, M, J, N and P.

Cut the Mouth from maroon felt. Sew one piece inside the lower teeth from A to A, following the line of stitching already there and matching centre fronts.

DRAGON — LIGHT RED FELT
Scale 1 square = 1"

Fill the chin with kapok. Stitch firmly through chin, filling, and inside mouth for 2in along centre line, as indicated by heavy broken line on pattern.

Sew the second mouth piece inside the upper teeth, from P to P. Fill the nose with kapok.

Cut the Horn from dark red felt. Make it up and sew it on to the nose in the same way as the spurs on arms and legs.

Stitch through the nose as you did the chin, along the centre line and around the horn as shown by the heavy broken line.

Neatly sew lower to upper lip each side from A to P.

Cut the Side Head pieces out of medium red felt. Sew the side head to chin, lips and back head, matching points Q, A, P, R, S, T and U.

Place the head over the wire, threading the tongue through the back of the mouth at O.

Sew chin to neck from Q to Q, matching centre line. Fill head with kapok and sew side head to neck from Q to U. Finish stuffing head firmly and sew up opening at back of head, U to U.

Form eyebrows by sewing through side and top head where shown on pattern, R to S.

Spine Cut the Spine from dark red felt, leaving no seam allowance along the long straight edge.

Seam along the jagged edge and then join each piece of spine, matching A to A, B to B etc. Trim and turn carefully.

Fill each individual triangle of spine with kapok, just enough to give it 'body' so that it will stand up. Sew from end to end of the spine along the dotted line. Place the spine on to the back seam of the dragon at X and pin into position. Pin upper spine to back seam of neck, stretching slightly if necessary to form a smooth line.

Sew the outside edges of the spine to the neck and continue to the top of the head at V, filling in with a little kapok where necessary.

Return to X and sew spine to body and tail, following the back seam and stretching and filling as necessary to give a smooth line. Finish off neatly at J.

Ears Cut the Ears from medium red felt and the Inner Ears from light red felt. Sew inner to outer ear along outside seam line, leaving the base open. Trim and turn and put in a little kapok. Turn in lower edges. Lay ear flat against side of head, with inner ear outwards, and sew to head along dotted line. Fold ear forward at W and sew securely to head.

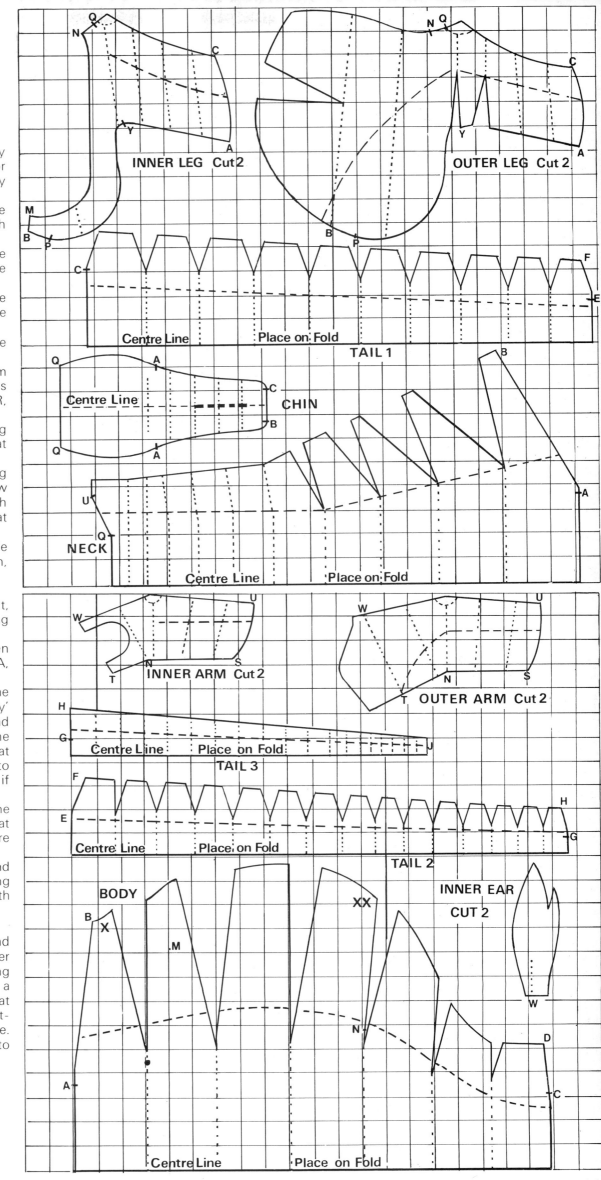

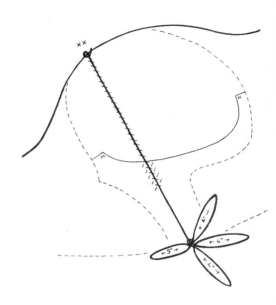

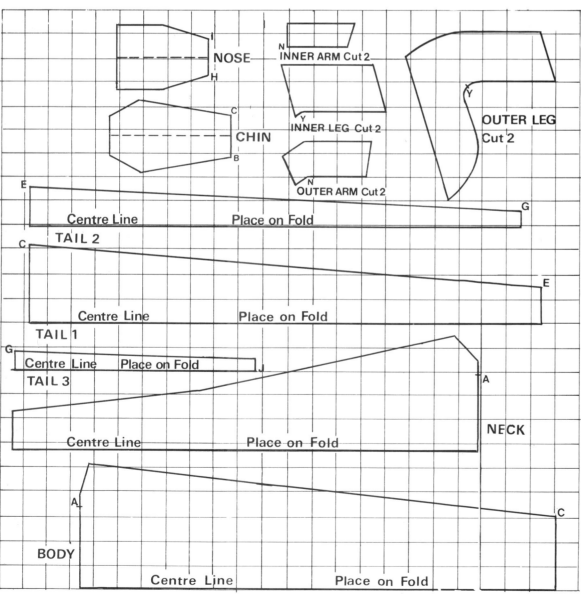

NOSE

INNER ARM Cut 2

CHIN

INNER LEG Cut 2

OUTER LEG
Cut 2

OUTER ARM Cut 2

E
Centre Line   Place on Fold   G

C
TAIL 2
Centre Line   Place on Fold   E

TAIL 1
G
Centre Line   Place on Fold   J

TAIL 3
A
Centre Line   Place on Fold

NECK

A

C

BODY
Centre Line   Place on Fold

Eyes Cut two circles from white felt and two smaller circles from black felt. Sew the black circles on the white ones as shown. Place the felt over the button, gather together at the back and fasten off securely.

If possible, it is a good idea to sew right through the head where the centre of the eyes will go, forming a shallow depression (or eye socket) each side of the head.

Place the eye well up under the brow and sew to the head.

Scales Cut Scales from medium red felt. The scales cover the back of the dragon from the spine to the tacked guide line, and the backs of the legs and arms to the guide line.

Most of these scales are 1in wide as shown on the pattern, but smaller scales are needed for the first 3in at the head end of the spine and the last 12in of the tail. Scaling the pattern down in size, cut some scales $\frac{1}{4}$in wide, some $\frac{1}{2}$in wide, and some $\frac{3}{4}$in wide.

Beginning at the end of the tail at J, sew a $\frac{1}{4}$in scale beside the spine. Sew the next $\frac{1}{4}$in scale $\frac{1}{4}$in above this, making sure the outside edge of the spine is covered Increase where there is room to $1\frac{1}{2}$ scales

DRAGON — WADDING AND LINING
Scale 1 square = 1"

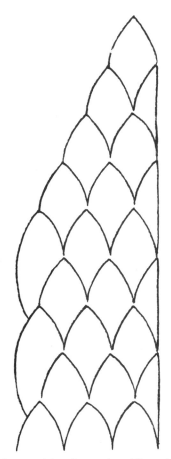

alternating with 1 scale. The half scale should lie next to the spine.

Still keeping between the spine and the guide line, increase the size of the scales to $\frac{1}{2}$in, with $\frac{1}{2}$in between the rows. Gradually increase the size of scales to $\frac{3}{4}$in and then to 1in.

Continue to sew on scales until you reach the base of the tail, overlapping and keeping a smooth edge as shown in diagram on page 45.

Using 1in scales and starting where the leg joins the foot, cover the back of the leg as far as the spur. Do the same on the arm. Returning to the base of the tail continue to cover the back and the top of the leg, curving the rows slightly to follow the shape where the leg merges into the back.

Cover the back and upper arm in the same way and continue up the neck to the head. Reduce the size of the scales until they are $\frac{1}{2}$in at V, the beginning of the spine, and finish off neatly.

Sew the scales on to the other side of the dragon. Remove all guide lines and press the scales with a steam iron or damp cloth.

DRAGON – ✳DARK RED FELT
✳✳ FLESH OR CREAM ✘MAROON FELT
■ BLACK FELT ✚WHITE FELT
Scale 1 square = 1"

DRAGON – MEDIUM RED FELT
Scale 1 square = 1"

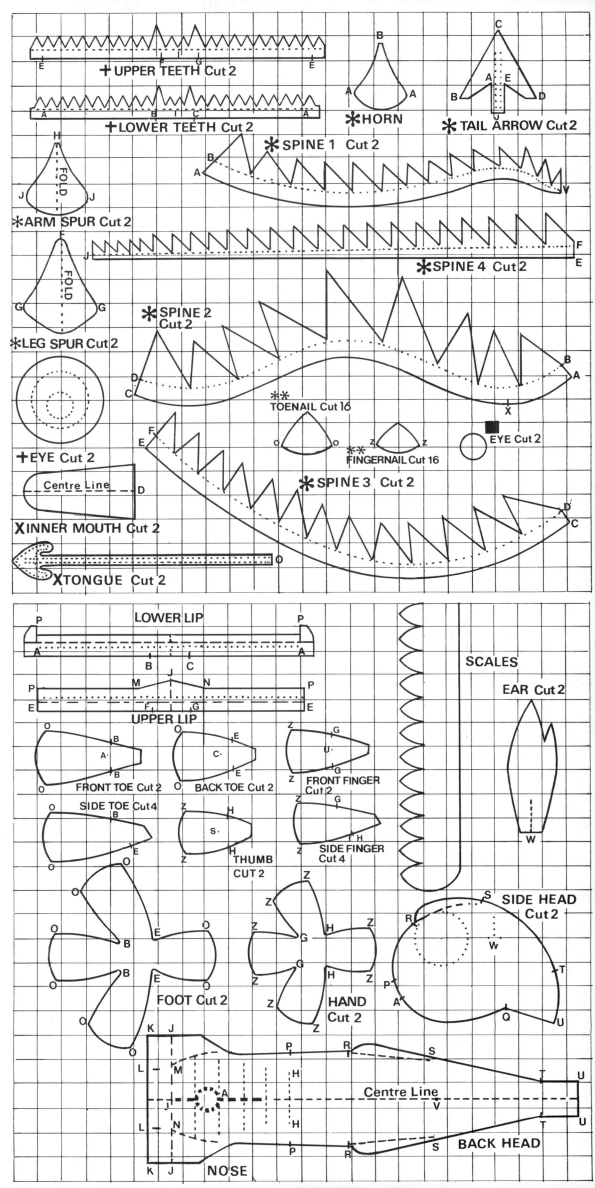

Basket Weaving

This chapter is intended for those of you who would like to try their hand at the ancient craft of basket weaving. The products of this craft make delightful gifts not only for friends, but also for yourself and your home.

Your hands will be your most important tool. All other equipment is of the simplest sort: an old pair of scissors or shears, an awl (or knitting-needle), a pail or large pan of water, and a large piece of plastic or some other suitable material to protect your working surface.

The material you will work with is known variously as rattan, cane, or wicker. It is available in most handicraft stores, and is sold in coils, by the pound. The amount of cane needed for each of the objects described will be indicated in the instructions.

As a rule, you will be working with two grades of cane. The frame or skeleton is constructed with fairly thick cane referred to as stakes; the actual weaving is done with somewhat thinner, more pliable cane, referred to as the weaver. The grade of cane needed (referred to by the symbol #) is also given in the instructions for each of the objects.

ROUND MAT *(below)*

For the lower round mat shown below, you will need 16 + 2 stakes, each 15in long, and 1½oz of # 3 weaver. Soak all the pieces for about five minutes in the water. (If you form a coil and fasten the ends with a clothespin, it should fit quite well into whatever container you use.)

Now place the 16 stakes crosswise as shown in figs. 1a and b (page 47). (Note the relative position of each of the groups of stakes.) Beginning underneath one group, bring a weaver four times, full circle, over and under as shown in fig. 1b, around the eight groups of stakes. Reverse direction, and bring the weaver around again four times full circle. Be sure that the weaver has been soaked long enough so that it is really pliable, or it may break during the step indicated in fig. 1c. Make sure that all the stakes are of equal length. If not, you can still adjust them at this point. Now divide the eight groups of stakes into sixteen pairs and insert the two additional stakes alongside of the pairs of stakes at the beginning of the ninth round of the weaver. (In the bottom photo on page 47 you can see how this addition is made.) This brings the number of pairs of stakes to 17. You must have an uneven number so that the over-and-under of the weaver alternates automatically as you proceed. This is the basic form on which nearly all of the other examples given in this chapter are based.

The most difficult part of the work is now finished. Continue weaving in the counter-clockwise direction established at fig. 1c. You will find it easiest to work at the edge of a table. Take care to keep the pairs of stakes evenly spaced. If you come to the end of a weaver, begin a new one under a stake as shown in fig. 1d. When the work reaches a diameter of 8in, insert the trimmed end of the weaver to a depth of 1in into the weave, parallel to the first stake (in other words, the stake under which the weaving process begins), as shown in fig. 1e. Trim the pairs of stakes to 3in, soak the entire piece for five minutes, and arch the right-hand stake of each pair to the right, inserting it about 1in deep into the weave parallel to the adjoining left-hand stake. Use the awl or knitting-needle to guide the end of the stakes into place. Trim the protruding left-hand stakes as shown.

Two alternate borders are shown on this page. The double arched border (top, left) is made as follows: after inserting the end of the weaver, as above, trim the pairs of stakes to approximately 4in (the right-hand one should be just a little shorter), soak the piece, and insert each pair of weavers about 1in deep into the weave, just to the left of the second pair of stakes, and not the pair immediately to the right. For the Madeira border (right), trim the stakes to 7in and weave each pair through the four adjoining pairs on the right (see page 47, top).

Allow the finished mat to dry thoroughly before trimming the ends (in the back), diagonally to the direction of the weave. You may protect it with a thin coat of clear spray shellac.

SNACK BASKET *(page 48, top)*

To make this snack basket, begin as for the round mat (see page 46). When the work reaches a diameter of 7in, draw firmly on the weaver until the stakes bend upward. Continue weaving to the desired height, and end the weave as for the mat. The double arched

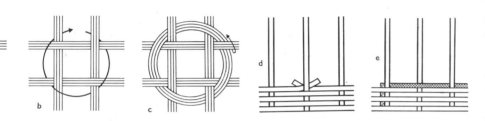

Fig. 1

border, a little shallower than the one shown on page 46, is appropriate for this basket.

Materials: 16+2 stakes, 20in long (# 6)
2½oz of weaver # 3

FRUIT BASKET
(page 48, bottom)

For the fruit basket, begin curving the stakes as soon as you begin the ninth round, and continue curving as you work to achieve the sloping edge. The photo clearly shows how the overlapping single arched border is made. The protruding stake may be trimmed just above the weaving edge or, as in the detail on the right of the photo, just above the curved stakes.

Materials: 16+2 stakes, 20in long (# 3)
1¾oz of weaver # 3

TRAYS *(page 49)*

Trays of all sizes and shapes are an indispensable aid to entertaining. You can make this elegant tray easily and inexpensively.

Handicraft shops supply prepared bases with holes punched all around the edge. Choose such a base 12×16in. (If you want to prepare the base yourself, take a piece of pressboard, veneer, or plywood, ⅛ to ¼in thick. Round off the edges and smooth with a file or sandpaper. Draw a line ¼in from the circumference, and along it mark 71 equidistant dots, at approximately ¾in intervals. Using a 1/16in bit, drill 71 holes as marked.)

Draw one soaked stake through each of the holes, allowing 2in to protrude on the underside of the base. Form these protruding ends into the foot of the tray like this: bring the first stake around the outside of the second, and flat along the inside of the third. Now bring the second stake around the outside of the third, and then back to the inside, as before (see photo, page 48, top right). Continue in this way until the foot is complete. To insert the last stake, loosen the first one gently with the knitting needle. Pull all the stakes upward until the foot comes to rest snugly against the base. Trim the ends on a diagonal, just beyond the point of adjacence to the third stake.

Begin the weaver on the inside of the tray, and weave ten rounds.

For the border, weave the first stake towards the inside around the second and third stakes, and then towards the outside around the fourth and fifth stakes, and finally insert it on the inside, parallel to the sixth stake. (We can abbreviate this procedure thus: two inside, two outside, fasten inside). You will thus be weaving the border towards the right.

Materials: 71 stakes, 8in long (# 5)
2⅘oz of weaver # 2

Another attractive method for edging a tray is clearly illustrated in the sequence of diagrams in fig. 3. You will need stakes 12in long to make this plaited border. In

47

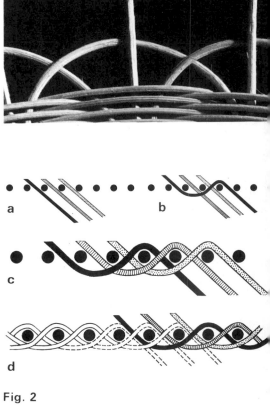

Fig. 2

bending the first two stakes forward, it is important to leave enough space for the eventual insertion of the last ones.

Another way of weaving the tray is to work with pairs of stakes. For this, the holes must be drilled with a $\frac{1}{8}$in bit, at $\frac{1}{2}$in intervals. For the foot, bring the first weaver inside around the second, outside around the third, and then inside along the fourth.

For the wall of the tray, proceed like this: Use three weavers, each one beginning on the inside of one of three adjoining pairs of stakes (see fig. 2a, page 48). Bring the first weaver around the outside of the first two pairs of stakes, above the other two weavers, around the inside of the third pair of stakes, and back outside again (see fig. 2b). Repeat this process with the other two weavers (see fig. 2c), and then again with the first weaver, continuing in this way for four complete rounds. Insert the end of each weaver parallel to the stake behind which it begins.

For the closed Madeira border, weave each pair of stakes in this sequence: outside, inside, outside, inside, outside, and inside parallel to the sixth pair of stakes. It is important to begin the weaving with the first pair of stakes high enough to leave room for insertion of the last pair of stakes when the round is completed.

Materials: 12 × 16in board with 95 holes
190 stakes in pairs, 8in long
(# 2) weaver # 2

This method of weaving is also appropriate for a circular tray. After five rounds with the weaver, make the border by weaving around four stakes rather than six.

Materials: circular board, 12in diameter, with 61 holes
122 stakes in pairs, 8in long
(# 2) weaver # 2

RATTAN LAMPSHADES AND WASTE BASKETS

Rattan lampshades add a look of easy elegance to any decor. Begin as you would for a tray. The board, of course, need not be strong—even stiff cardboard will do. A good size for lamps is 5in in diameter and 7in high. The board is held in place by a knot in the electrical cord, which is drawn through a hole in its centre.

Beginning with a prepared base, and weaving as for a tray, but with walls of appropriate size, you can make a number of objects such as wastebaskets, holders for wine bottles, and jardinieres.

If you prefer to weave the bottom as well, you might like to try one of the wastebaskets shown on page 50 (top). The largest one of these is made with a prepared base, but the other two have woven bottoms. Both of them are reinforced at the edge of the base (that is, just after the stakes are bent upwards) with one round of triple weave

Fig. 3

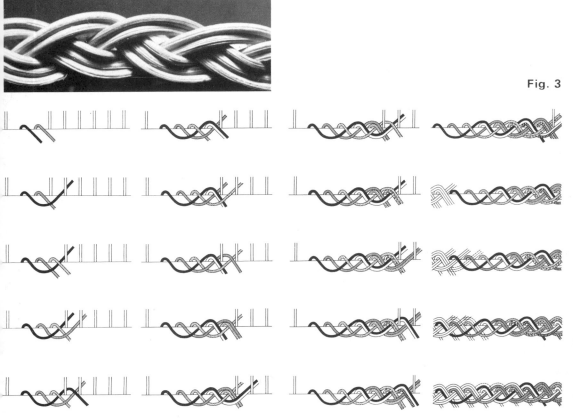

(see fig. 2d, page 48). This reinforcing should be done with a weaver of the same grade as the stakes. You will find it easier to shape the basket if you work around a container (such as a large metal canister) of the appropriate size.

For the right-hand basket, use a pair of weavers at the bottom. Before the round of triple weave at the edge, insert 17 new stakes alongside the original stakes and 1in into the weave of the bottom. Trim the original stakes as close as possible to the bottom edge. The interesting texture is achieved by a process known as pairing, that is, weaving simultaneously with two pairs of weavers which are alternately brought around each stake, one pair inside and one outside each successive stake. The border at the top is woven one outside, one inside, one outside, close off inside.

Materials: Left Basket: 25 stakes, 22in long (# 16)
21oz of weaver # 11
prepared base: 9in diameter (border: two inside, one outside close inside)

Centre Basket: 16+2 stakes, 30in long (# 6)
7¾oz of weaver # 4 (woven base: 8in diameter)

Right Basket: 8+1 stakes, 10in long (# 8)
for bottom: 17 stakes, 22in long (# 8)
for side: 14oz of weaver # 3 (woven base: 9in diameter)

The charming and useful basket on page 51 (top) is quite simple to make. Weave the base as usual. When the work reaches a diameter of 5in or 6in, bend the stakes at right angles and weave the sides. (Of course, the piece should be soaked well. Still it may happen that the stakes crack a little when bent at right angles—this is all right). Weave the cover a few rounds larger than the base.

Materials: Base: 16+2 stakes, 14in long (# 2)
Lid: 16+2 stakes, 12in long (# 2)
Both parts: 2¼oz of weaver # 2

The jardiniere on page 50 (bottom) is easily made, either with a prepared base or with a woven bottom.

HI-JACKS *(colour picture, page 51)*
'Hi-jacks' are both attractive and more useful than coasters, since they are carried around with the glass. They can be as simple or as ornate as you like. You need only ½oz of material for each one. The stakes should be # 1, the weavers # 0 or # 00. Instead of the basic 16+2 stakes, you may use 8+2 (as for the right-hand hi-jacks below).

t is not necessary to make the 4 + 4 rounds
described on page 46; instead, you may
immediately begin alternate weaving over
pairs of stakes. Allow all hi-jacks to dry on
the glass, in order to keep the proper shape
and size.

SHALLOW FRUIT BASKET
(page 52, top)

For a shallow fruit basket, weave the
bottom in the usual manner to a diameter of
8in. Separate the pairs of stakes into single
stakes and insert one additional stake 1in
deep into the weave between two of the
original stakes. When the work reaches a
diameter of 11in or 12in, make a triple weave
edge as shown in fig. 2d, page 48, and
weave the side to a height of 1in (about 17
rounds). The border described on page 53,
and fig. 4, is well suited for this basket.

Materials: 16 + 2 stakes, 30in long (# 6)
         1 stake, 14in long (# 6)
         4½oz of weaver # 3

JARDINIERE *(page 54, bottom left)*

To show off your favourite house plant, you
can make the attractive jardiniere in the
guise of a flower basket. The bottom is woven
with one weaver to a diameter of 5in, and
the sides, after an edge of triple weave (see
fig. 2d, page 48), are woven with a pair of
weavers. The handle is twisted of two lengths
of cane, inserted through the weave of the
lower part of the basket (on the inside) as far
as the bottom, and fastened on the outside
with natural colour raffia.

Materials: 16 + 2 stakes, 32in long (# 8)
         5oz of weaver # 5
         two 56in lengths of # 13 cane
         (for handle)

BABY RATTLES *(page 52, bottom left)*

The material used for the baby rattles is very
thin, and need therefore be soaked only for
a short time. After the fourth round, begin
shaping the work to a round or pear shape,
continuing to shape it with the left hand as
you weave. Insert a few old coins or pebbles
before closing the shape for the handle. Cut
away about half the stakes 1in from the body
of the rattle. Bend the remaining stakes into
a loop, and wind the entire handle with a
single weaver.

Materials: 16 + 2 stakes, 26—28in long (# 0
         or # 1)
         ½oz of weaver # 00 or # 000

MORE LAMPSHADES

You can make an attractive lamp by covering
an empty wine or liquor bottle with rattan.
Tie 7 stakes to the neck of the bottle and
proceed to weave (see the top, right-hand
photo on page 53). Light fixtures and lampshades can be found in department and hardware stores. You can also buy a lampshade
frame and cover it yourself with fabric or
parchment.

Materials: 7 stakes, 14in long (# 6)
weaver # 3

For greater ease in shaping a small lamp-shade, work around a bottle of suitable form, such as a Chianti bottle. Tie 9 pairs of stakes to the neck of the bottle and proceed to weave. To vary the shape, tie layers of newspaper smoothly over the bottle and weave over the shape thus produced. Work the stakes at both ends into simple borders.

Materials: 18 stakes, 18in long (# 6)
weaver # 3

The attractive lampshades on page 52 (bottom right) and page 53 (bottom left) are freehand. The one on page 52 is woven to a slightly flared cylindrical shape after the first eight (4 + 4) rounds for about 3in.

Materials: 16 + 2 stakes, 32in long (# 5)
$5\frac{3}{4}$oz of weaver # 3

For the lampshade on the left, tie 23 stakes around a glass jar or a tin can, leaving about 7in of the stakes protruding at the top. After weaving a few rounds, remove the jar or can and continue weaving, shaping the shade freely as you work. For the neck, work around a flower pot of appropriate size. Trim the centre stake of each group of three to the weaving edge, and form the open pattern by joining the right-hand stake of each pair with the left-hand stake of the adjoining pair. After nine rounds of weaving, form the border at the top in the same manner as at the bottom, but in reverse direction: one inside, one outside, close off inside.

Materials: 69 stakes, 22in long (# 3)
5oz of weaver # 1

OPENWORK BASKET
(page 53, bottom right)
For this graceful openwork basket, weave the base a little concave rather than entirely flat, to a diameter of 7in. Insert 17 new stakes between the original 17 pairs. Form an arch with each of the groups of three to a height of $3\frac{1}{2}$in, interweave as shown, and plait at the base as follows: working clock-wise, bring one group to the right and under-neath the next one, over the third, and inside along the fourth. When the round is completed, pull all the ends snug so that the plait lies smooth and trim.

Materials: 16 + 2 stakes, 48in long (# 6)
17 stakes, 22in long (# 6)
$3\frac{1}{4}$oz of weaver # 3

OVAL BASKET *(page 54, top)*
For the oval basket, form the crosspiece with pairs of stakes ($\frac{3}{16}$in apart on the length and

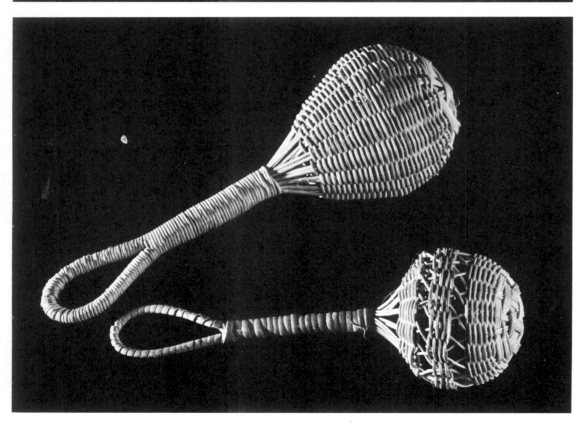

$\frac{1}{2}$in apart on the width) and begin immediately with rounds of alternate weave (that is, omitting the 4+4 rows of even weaving). Begin weaving·the sides when the base reaches a width of 4in.

Materials: 10 stakes, 20in long (# 5)
12+2 stakes, 16in long (# 5)
$2\frac{1}{2}$oz of weaver # 3

Figure 4 on page 55, illustrates the method for the border suggested for the shallow fruit basket (page 52) and the knitting basket (page 54, right). Begin by bringing 3 stakes forward, each one behind the two adjoining stakes. Now bring the first stake in front of the next two and behind the one after that. You have now finished working with the first stake, and you must leave it as it is until the very end, when you will trim it as closely as possible. Now, counting the fourth upright stake as the third, repeat the process as with the first three, and so on until the border is completed.

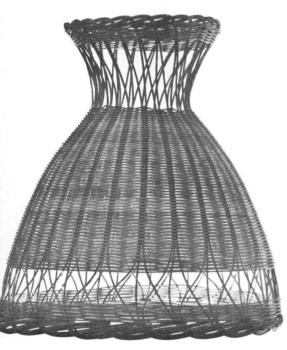

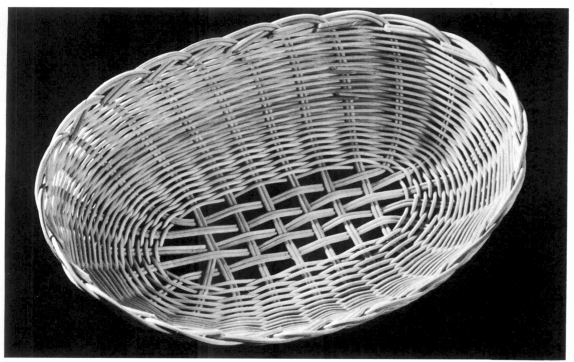

KNITTING BASKET *(page 54, right)*

For the knitting basket, weave a flat base to a diameter of 5in. Separate the pairs of stakes and make a triple weave foot (see fig. 2d, page 48), working with the now single stakes. Form the curve which joins bottom and side as follows: push the stakes inward with the thumb and forefinger of the left hand, holding the weaver in place at the same time. When the sides are 4in high, weave the border described on page 53. For the handle, point the ends of the cane and insert them directly opposite each other through the border and 2in down into the weave, each alongside a pair of stakes. Fasten one end of the handle by crisscrossing with a weaver, having the beginning of the weaver lying alongside the handle. Wind the handle firmly with the weaver, and fasten the other end of the handle in the same manner as the first, pushing the end of the weaver up through the last winding, and drawing it taut.

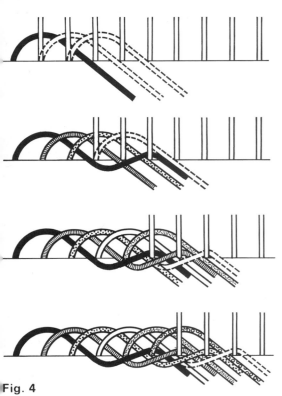

Materials: 16+2 stakes, 26in long (# 6)
4oz of weaver # 3
¼in thick cane, 32in long (for
handle)

MIRROR FRAME (below left)

This attractive and unusual mirror frame is
much easier to make than you would suspect.
Begin weaving as for the round mat (page 46)
to a diameter of 9in, using the # 5 weaver.
Separate the pairs of stakes and continue
weaving around the single stakes plus one
(to keep the uneven number) to a diameter
of 12in. Insert the 35 new stakes alongside
the original 35 and bend only these new ones
upward. They will form the support for the
mirror. Place the mirror onto the woven base
and conceal the edge of the mirror by
pairing with # 3 weaver (see page 50).

Edge with one outside, one inside, one outside, close off inside. Finally, weave 6
rounds of pairing (# 3 weaver) around the
35 original stakes, finishing with a border
of single overlapping arches.

Materials: 16+2+1 stakes, 24in long (# 8)
35 stakes, 8in long (# 6)
5¾oz of weaver # 5 and # 3
circular mirror, 12in diameter,
¼in thick

Save the left-over pieces of rattan. They can
be fashioned into delightful, imaginative
mobiles such as the fish, below left, and the
sailboat, below right. For the boat, tie three
or five lengths of rattan to form the hull, and
attach the mast and struts as shown. Indicate
the sails with string, raffia, or pieces of thin
rattan glued to the struts as shown.

Fig. 4

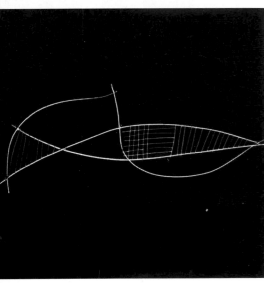

Working with Leather

When we engage in handicrafts, it does not really matter what materials we choose to work with. For in any creative endeavour, the essential element is the joy of seeing an idea take tangible shape under our own hands—and the pleasure of giving the work of our own hands to a friend.

This chapter on leathercraft justifies its own existence in two ways. First, working with leather requires little equipment (most of it noiseless!). Second—and this is by far more important—leather transmits a vivid impression of the living, the genuine, the organic. It is not surprising, then, that in this age of synthetics, so many people appreciate genuine leather. Only leather is leather! No matter how good an imitation is, it cannot replace leather. How pronounced, for example, is the inimitable smell of leather!

We have one earnest plea to the reader: do not make exact copies of the leather objects shown in this chapter. Make some small but original variation, or use a given form of ornamentation on another object. What is the reason for this advice? It is only in this way—and not by slavish adherence to the examples given—that you will gain confidence, develop good judgement in matters of taste, and be truly justified in the pride you will have for the objects you create.

The most prosaic object—a corkscrew, a pair of scissors, a ball point pen—becomes a desirable gift when it is presented in its own handmade leather case. The examples shown on this page and page 57 (top) are quickly and easily (and inexpensively!) made from small pieces of leather left over from bigger projects.

The knife case (bottom, left) is made of a wide strip of grey leather with white lacing. The perforated loops of olive green leather are skived at the ends (see picture B, page 61, for instructions on skiving) and glued in place on the inside of the case before lacing.

The pen and pencil case (page 56, centre) is made of two basic pieces (front and back, cut separately) of tan leather. It is equipped with a loop woven of narrow strips of tan and brown leather (see fig. 16, page 62), and the edges are joined with saddle stitch (see picture C, page 61).

The scissors case (page 56, bottom right) is of the simplest design, but the alternate spiral lacing adds a more elaborate touch. Actually, this lacing is very simple; it is just a question of positioning every other slit or hole in the leather slightly further away from the edge.

The change purse (page 57, top centre) is equipped with a snap fastener. A kit with snap fasteners in a variety of colours and sizes, and the necessary tool, is available in department stores. The pattern for this purse is given in fig. 16, page 62.

Lacing instructions and diagrams are given on page 61.

The thumbsize manikin (page 57, top left) could add a touch of humour to a rather sober office or study. You might like to add cuphooks at the top and the bottom, and suspend several of them in a chain to liven up a dull corner. Instructions are given in fig. 15 on page 62.

A pair of brass bookends covered with leather, such as the one shown on page 57, top right, would make a welcome gift for your favourite scholar or executive. The upright surface measures 5 × 7in; the 'foot' is 4in long, and does not have a leather covering. The stark geometric shapes are carefully cut out with a stencil knife and the leather pieces are then laced to the metal which has first of all been protected with a coat of shellac.

Magazine rack If you have had any experience with woodworking, you can easily make a magazine rack such as the one opposite. (Or you can ask one of your woodworking friends to help you.) The frame is made of four bow-shaped pieces of wood of equal size, three dowels (beechwood is a good choice), and two carved nails. As you can see from the photo, this project can provide you with a lot of opportunity for experimenting with ornamental lacing.

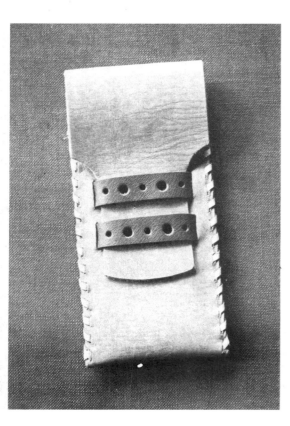
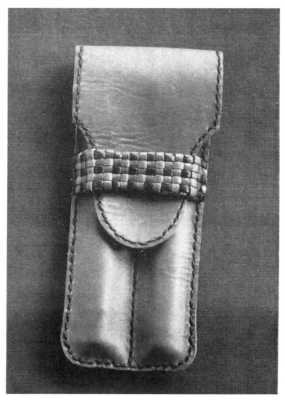
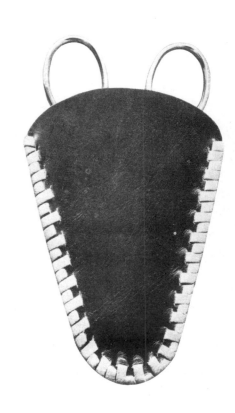

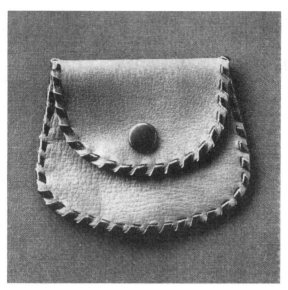

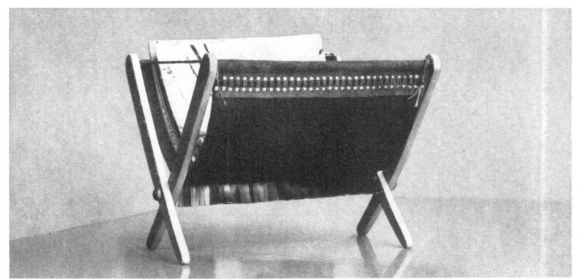

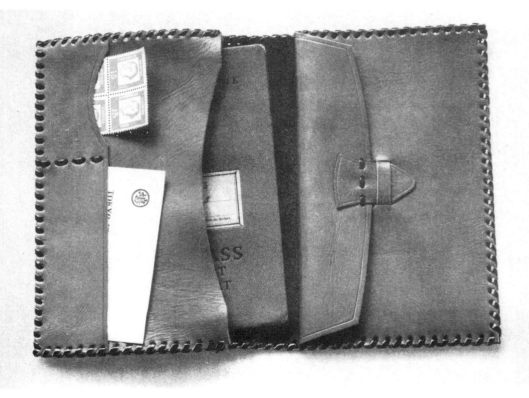

Book cover Another gift for the lover of books is a handmade leather book cover. The actual construction is very simple, and sometimes (especially in the case of well-grained leather) the only ornamentation is added in the lacing. A smooth leather, such as calfskin, might be enhanced by the addition of a design lightly burned on with a soldering iron (see page 57, bottom right). The design must consist of straight lines, since the soldering iron is drawn along a metal ruler. To avoid injuring the leather, round the tip of the iron slightly with a file. An interesting effect can be obtained if strips of leather in a contrasting colour are laced through horizontal and diagonal slits on the front of the book. It is a good idea to practice this technique beforehand with paper.

In making a wallet, there are several things to consider, namely the size, the practicality of the various compartments, and the adequate thickness of the leather. Once you have resolved these questions, you can apply yourself to the rewarding task of exercising your sense of design. To make sure that you will have an even lacing job, you should fasten the edges to be joined with adhesive (rubber cement is good) before punching the holes or slits. The wallet (page 57, bottom left) is made of medium brown calfskin. The measurements are given in fig. 17, page 62.

Never try to imitate nature to the point of deceptive similarity. Rather, let the material you are working with keep its own character. **The leather flower** on the right demonstrates this principle very well. The 'rose' is made of red and grey nappa leather. The stem is made of heavy copper wire, the tip of which is hooked through a large, leather-covered wooden bead to form the centre of the flower. The 'stamens' are fringes of leather shirred on a strong thread. Leather adhesive, available in handicraft shops, is used.

Handbag The technique of embossing leather is described on page 61. The possibilities for design are virtually limitless. Once you begin exploring this technique, you will no doubt find yourself returning to it. The handsome bag on this page, bottom left, shows an example of embossing. It is made of two pieces of leather 10 × 12in, each embossed. The two halves are placed with the right sides (embossed sides) together and seamed at bottom and sides. Then the bag is turned right side out. It may be equipped with a spring-type mechanism which opens to a square and closes flat. A leather button and loops will do equally well to secure the opening. Two steel rings holding the straps of braided leather laces, and a lining of taffeta, complete the bag.

The unusual leather napkin rings (page 59, top) provide an excellent opportunity for the beginner in leathercraft to explore his

talents, to experiment with ideas, and to practice a number of useful techniques. Scraps of thin, soft leather are used for this project, so if any is spoiled, not much is lost.

Make a cardboard ring by wrapping several layers of thin cardboard around a straight-sided bottle or jar of the appropriate size, securing the ends with glue or tape. Now cut a strip of thin, supple leather about 1 in longer than the circumference of the cardboard ring, and not quite twice as wide. Ornament this leather strip down the centre with decorative lacing, wooden or ceramic beads, fringes—whatever you like. You might use any of the ideas shown in the picture as a starting point, but let your own imagination be your guide. (The various lacing techniques are illustrated and described on page 61). Glue the finished leather strip to the cardboard ring, skiving the overlapping ends as well as the edges. (The technique of skiving is described and illustrated on page 61.) Rubber cement is the best adhesive to use in this case, because it dries slowly, allowing you to make adjustments and correct errors. Finally, cut another strip of leather, again 1 in longer than the circumference of the ring, and $\frac{1}{4}-\frac{1}{2}$ in narrower, skive the overlapping ends and the edges, and glue in place as the lining of the ring.

The necklace has always had a favoured place in the history of jewelry. In earlier times, jewelry was made almost exclusively of bone, metal and precious or semi-precious stones. Nowadays, wood, ceramic, glass, synthetics are used—to name but a few materials. The use of leather for making necklaces and other body ornaments has only recently achieved great popularity. As you see on page 58, this material can be very effectively used to make elegant neck-

aces. Instructions for making the leather 'beads' and tassels of these necklaces are given in fig. 14, page 62. You will find plenty of ideas for creating your own leather jewelry by looking at examples of American Indian and Greenlandic leather ornaments in a museum of folk crafts.

Mirrors are as much decorative pieces as they are useful accessories in the home. A handmade leather frame provides an elegant accent for any decor. The rectangular frame of green leather (page 60, bottom left) is deceptively easy to make. Instructions are given in fig. 18, page 62.

Desk accessories You can make attractive desk and bureau accessories by covering boxes and containers of all sorts with nappa leather. These covers can be as plain or elaborate as you wish. The knitting box on page 61, bottom right, is made with just one colour of leather and a very simple design. On the other hand, you can make a rather taller pencil holder which is a little more ornate. Actually, the design is easy, if somewhat painstaking, to create. Having cut a piece of leather of appropriate size to cover the container you have chosen (a tin can is fine), allowing a little extra for over-lapping at the seam and at top and bottom, punch holes along the top and the bottom in a symetrical frieze pattern. Glue a thin piece of fabric behind the leather, and replace the punched-out portions with tiny circles punched from a piece of leather in a con-trasting colour. Cover the container, folding the leather under at the bottom and inside at the top. Line the container with fabric, felt, or self-adhesive ('contact') paper.

The elephant shown on page 59 is not difficult to make. See the instructions in fig. 19, page 62. Its particular charm lies in the fact that his tusks are made of real bone. You can saw and file thoroughly dried bones from your Sunday roast to the size and shape required. Of course, hardwood makes an adequate substitute.

A leather-covered bottle makes an attractive lamp base, such as the one on page 60, right. Fill the bottle with fine sand and insert the electrical fixture (available in hardware stores). A lampshade of genuine parchment adds the right touch of elegance.

THE TYPES OF LEATHER

Many factors influence the specific grade and quality of leather. First of all, it may be tanned by one of three methods: with organic compounds, with mineral com-pounds, or with synthetic compounds. Leather may have a pronounced natural grain, or, as in the case of very thick steer-hide, it may be split and artificially grained. It may be smooth and supple (such as suede or doeskin), or quite heavy and stiff (such as steerhide or pigskin). It may be coloured superficially (sprayed), or with a penetrating dye. Finally, the age, sex, and health of the

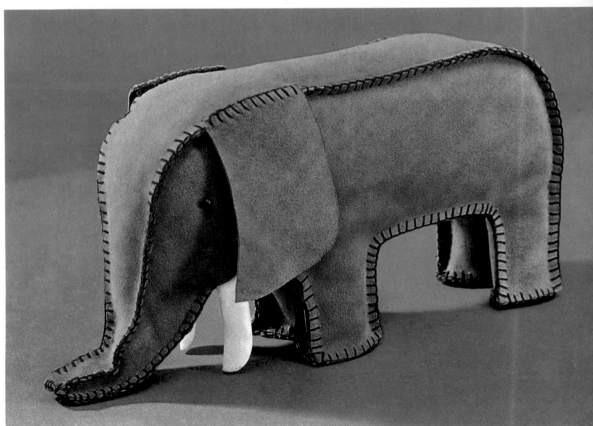

animal from whose hide the leather is made has a good deal of influence on the quality of the leather.

In choosing leather, let your own sense of touch be the first guide, and after that, rely on the advice of your dealer.

Here is a brief description of each of the most common types of leather.

Steerhide is relatively stiff and tough. Split steerhide is recommended for the first attempts at such projects as the cases and purses shown on pages 56 and 57.

Calfskin has a finer grain and is more flexible. It is ideal for handbags, and for all embossed work.

Goatskin is supple and extremely soft, and can be shirred like fabric. It is ideal for covering boxes and other containers.

Sheepskin is very similar to goatskin, except that it is usually somewhat thicker, and looser in texture. It is often used as a lining.

Pigskin has the most pronounced grain. It is valued for its characteristic appearance and its durability.

The first four types of leather are known collectively as nappa leather if they have been treated by a special emollient tanning process.

HINTS FOR BUYING LEATHER

The best source for leather is a handicraft shop. There are also leather supply houses. Department stores, too, sometimes carry a small stock of leather in the fabrics department. When you have had some practice in leathercraft, you might consider buying an entire hide. You will find that the back portion of the hide is uniform in quality and in thickness, the neck portion is relatively thick, and the stomach portion relatively thin. Thus you will have three different grades of leather, which you may cut to whatever shapes you need. Small imperfections and noticeable irregularities in the grain are characteristic of leather: you must take them into account, and not be unduly fastidious in choosing your material.

Goatskin laces about $\frac{1}{8}$ in wide are available by the yard in a variety of colours, again in handicraft shops or leather supply houses. You may also prepare the laces yourself from a circle of thin leather in the desired colour. Beginning at the outside, cut in a spiral shape towards the centre, taking care to keep the strip at an even width.

TOOLS AND GLUE

Here is a list of basic tools used in leathercraft: a lacing chisel (for punching slits in the leather prior to lacing): a rotary punch (you can make holes of different sizes with this): a mat knife or well-sharpened paring knife (cut all straight edges of the leather with a knife drawn along a metal ruler; it makes a cleaner edge than do scissors): a metal 'T'-square, scissors (for curved edges and for cutting laces): a tracing wheel (this is handy for marking the edge of the leather at uniform intervals for punching); a stencil knife or linoleum cutter for cutting within the leather (see the book-end, page 57); a mallet or hammer for embossing; and a soldering iron (for burning designs into the leather, as in the book cover, page 57).

For ordinary adhering in leathercraft use any good, quick-drying glue. For a stronger, flexible bond use the special leather glue available in the handicraft shop (this is a type of vegetable glue). Finally, if you want to be able to undo and adjust the work, use rubber cement.

THE CARE OF TOOLS

Most of the basic tools listed above require a minimum of care. However, any knives that you use—stencil knife, mat knife, paring knife, skiving knife—should be well sharpened to begin with, and periodically stropped on a knife sharpener or on a leather razor strop. A dull knife slows down the work, makes it less enjoyable, and tends to produce untidy results.

BASIC TECHNIQUES OF LEATHERCRAFT
Cutting the Leather:

All straight edges in leathercraft can be cut with a knife drawn along a metal ruler. The thicker the leather, the more important it is to hold the knife at a perfect right angle to it. Draw the knife carefully towards

yourself while holding the ruler firmly in place with the spread fingers of your left hand (see A, left). Always have the piece to be used to the left of the knife so that, should the knife slip, you have not spoiled that piece. Protect the surface of your worktable with heavy cardboard.

Skiving:

If you are covering an object with leather— a napkin ring, for example, or a container— there will be an unsightly joint where the ends overlap. To avoid this, both ends of the leather should be skived. Place the leather face down on your working surface and, using a skiving knife or other sharp, wide-bladed knife, 'shave' off thin layers off the edge of the leather with sawing motions.

The Saddle Stitch:

This is the common method of joining two pieces of leather. It is actually an ordinary running stitch made with two threads at the same time (picture C, top right). For best results, use two needles, stitch the first from front to back and the second from back to front, pull both threads taut; now stitch the first from back to front and the second from front to back, pull both threads taut; repeat process until the entire seam is made. Heavy waxed linen thread for use in leathercraft is available in handicraft shops. (You will find the work much easier if you punch very small holes in both leather pieces with an awl before proceeding to sew).

EMBOSSING

This is one of the most interesting techniques for ornamenting leather. An endless variety of effects can be achieved by stamping the dampened leather with shapes cut from pinewood lathes, or made by filing down large nailheads. Figure B, below right shows some examples. Use a small hammer or mallet to impress these shapes into the leather. A small plywood board placed underneath the leather during the embossing process helps in producing deep, clear impressions. The handbag on page 58 shows examples of embossing with pinewood shapes. The wooden stamps should be briefly soaked in water and dried again before being used.

ORNAMENTAL LACING

(figs. 1–12 above)

If you want a more elaborate edge for your leatherwork than the one produced by the simple saddle stitch, you can make use of any of the methods of lacing. Prepare the leather by making evenly spaced holes in the edges of the leather, either with a lacing chisel, which makes slits, or with a punch. A tracing wheel run lightly along the edge is handy for marking equidistant holes. There is also a type of punch available which, as it punches one hole, marks the one follow-

 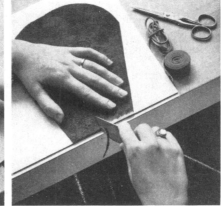 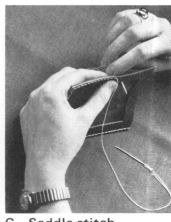

A Cutting   B Skiving   C Saddle stitch

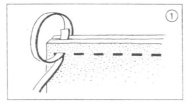 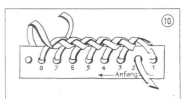 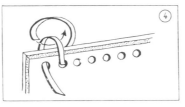
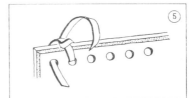 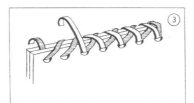 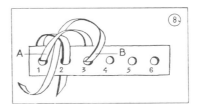
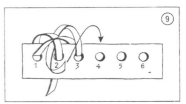 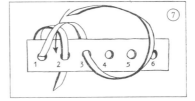 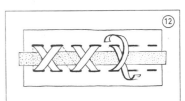
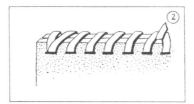 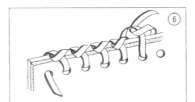 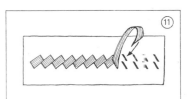

Figs. 1—12   **Fig. 13**

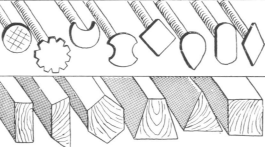

ing. To make the lacing easier, trim the end of the lace on the diagonal to a point.

Spiral or Whipstitch *(figs. 1–2):*
This is the simplest lacing stitch. It consists of running a single lace, spiral fashion, through successive holes in the edge of the leather. Sometimes the concealing of

the ends of the lace causes a problem. One way of solving this is always to make the first and the last loop a double one. If you are joining two pieces of leather, conceal the ends of the lace between them. If you are edging a single layer, it is best to skive the ends and glue them to the leather. If you must add on a new piece of lace because the first is too short, skive the ends to be joined, and paste them together with leather adhesive, overlapping about $\frac{3}{4}$ in.

Cross Stitch *(fig. 3)*:
Simply lace the entire piece with spiral stitch, and then bring another lace in the same manner through the same holes, but in the opposite direction. You might experiment with laces in two different colours.

Buttonhole Stitch *(figs. 4–6)*:
The principle of this stitch, is probably familiar to everyone. The diagrams clearly illustrate the technique.

Braid Stitch *(figs. 7–10)*:
This stitch is less familiar than the buttonhole stitch, but just as easy to do, and the effect is richer. Only the first three stitches need particular attention; the rest is easy. Place the leather face down. Beginning at the back, draw a lace through the second hole towards the front, then back to front through the first, and finally, back to front, through the third (fig. 7). The result is a pair of crisscrossed loops, through which you now draw the lace, again back to front (fig. 8). With the left hand, draw the lace taut at the place marked A, and with the right hand at the place marked B. Allow the last loop to remain loose. Now bring the lace through the fourth hole, back to front (fig. 9), creating a new pair of loops. Proceed as before, drawing the lace taut in the places mentioned, after each stitch. Figure 10 shows the actual view of the work from the front. To make the beginning and end of the braid stitch lacing flow smoothly into one another, loosen the first three or four stitches gently and draw the loose end through the resulting loops. To lace around a corner, make one complete, three-part stitch through the same hole.

Ornamental Lacing, Staggered *(fig. 11)*:
Apart from the precise placement of the slits, this stitch presents no difficulties. By adding another row of slits and lacing in the opposite direction, you can produce a herring-bone pattern.

Ornamental Lacing, Crisscross *(fig. 12)*:
This stitch was used for the napkin ring with beads on page 59, and for the leather-covered bottle on page 60. The similarity of this technique with the simple procedure of lacing a shoe is unmistakable.

Fig. 14
The various elements of the necklace shown on page 63 are shown at a, b and c at the right. For added contrast, alternate the rough and smooth sides of the leather towards the outside. Part e is made from a strip of leather wound around the tassel and the loop. A 'leather button' necklace (not illustrated) can be made by joining the links shown in f and g.

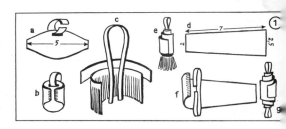

Fig. 15
The basic form for the doll on page 57 is a length of dowel. Shape the head with a knife and sand-paper (see a). Cut the garment patterns from paper first (b=dress, c=sleeve). Use wooden beads for the hands. Trim with fringes (d) as desired. For the hat, wind a leather lace into a spiral (e). Make the wig according to pattern f.

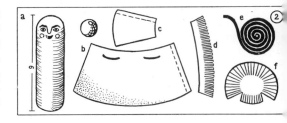

Fig. 16
The pattern for the change purse on page 57, top centre, is given at the right. Cut the shape from thin cardboard. The third sketch illustrates the method for weaving the 'tongue' for the pen and pencil case on page 56. Place a strip of leather behind the weaving, and bring the lace behind it after each row of crossweaving.

Fig. 17
Calfskin or split steerhide are appropriate materials for the wallet on page 57. Cut the pattern for each piece from cardboard first, and arrange on the leather in order to cut in the most economical way. You may add the two vee-shaped gussets which will permit further opening of the passport compartment. This, of course, is an optional feature.

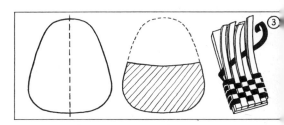

Fig. 18
For the mirror frame on page 60, first make a wooden frame of smooth laths (b). Arrange cardboard shapes (three examples at d, another at a) all around the frame and glue in place. Cut pattern c from leather. Spread adhesive on wood, cardboard shapes, and back of leather. Press leather in place, first along edges A and C, and then across the front (at B).

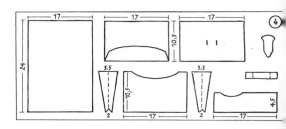

Fig. 19
For the elephant on page 59, cut a paper pattern in the desired size. Cut shape a twice out of leather. Between the two sides, you will need leather pieces b (= back and hind legs) and c (= throat and front legs). Cut two pieces according to the shaded area of a, and join as in d. The legs are three-sided. The sole of the foot is shown at e, the ears at f, tusk at g and tail at h.

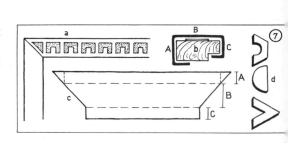

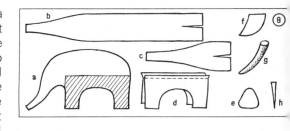

Mobiles

Since its introduction by Alexander Calder in the 1930s, the mobile has gained popularity with unusual speed. Perhaps this art form has been received so enthusiastically because it offers, by its very nature, a kind of antidote to the restlessness and materialism of modern life. It has no other purpose than to delight the eye. The mobile, as everyone knows, is a delicately balanced construction of wire and various shapes suspended by nearly invisible threads. Normal air currents cause these shapes to remain in constant motion. The possibilities for making a mobile are almost without limit. Since it is the purpose of this chapter to encourage you to make your own mobiles, only a few examples are shown, to introduce you to these possibilities. By a certain logic, bird, fish and boat shapes occur most frequently as motifs, since the motion of the mobile is most like that of swimming or flying. But these popular preferences should not limit you. Thus we include here instructions for a goose-girl, and her flock, Snow White and the Seven Dwarfs, as well as some abstract constructions. Since a properly constructed mobile is almost constantly in motion, it is difficult to photograph. Still, there are a few photographs of finished mobiles, although most of the illustrations show the separate elements of various mobiles, so that you may see the details of their construction. A mobile is not hard to make, and your finished product will not fail to give you pleasure. And don't forget that a mobile makes a delightful present.

HERE'S HOW IT'S DONE:

There is only one basic principle in the construction of a mobile, namely, that all the parts be able to move freely and without touching one another. The problem of balance is not nearly as difficult as might be expected.

To construct a mobile, begin at the bottom. Cut a piece of wire about eight inches (15–20cm) long and, with fine-nosed pliers, bend the ends upwards to form small loops, from which you will suspend the first two figures. Attach a length of thread near the centre of the wire, adjusting it until the wire is balanced horizontally. Keep the thread in place with a drop of strong adhesive, such as Duco Cement. Now suspend this construction from one of the loops in a second piece of wire, somewhat longer than the first. Hang another figure on the other loop. Balance the whole construction from the second wire and fasten the thread as before. Repeat this procedure three or four times, as you wish, and depending on the size of mobile you have in mind. The top wire will be considerably longer than the others. From one of its loops the whole construction is suspended, and from the other, suspend another figure either on a very short or on a very long thread. Be sure to arrange all the figures in such a way that they cannot collide.

The basic pattern shown in fig. 1, page 64, is quite long and would therefore be particularly suitable for a high-ceilinged room.

For a mobile which is wide rather than long, suspend two similar constructions from both ends of the top wire.

If your figures are made of straw, paper or other lightweight material, use a fine grade of steel wire. For heavier figures, use brass or copper wire. Always use the thinnest grade of wire possible: that is, it must be strong enough to support the figures without bending appreciably. To suspend the figures, a thin nylon thread is most suitable as it is practically invisible. A heavy nylon thread will tend to restrict the movement of the figures. Ordinary sewing thread may also be used.

The chicken (page 64, top centre) is folded from paper cut according to fig. 2, page 65. Join the flaps as indicated. When hanging the individual figures, balance the chicken so that her head is a little higher. If you want to make a rooster, the tail is not cut with the basic shape, but is attached at the end—a fine bunch of colourful paper strips. Finally, paint comb, feet and beak red.

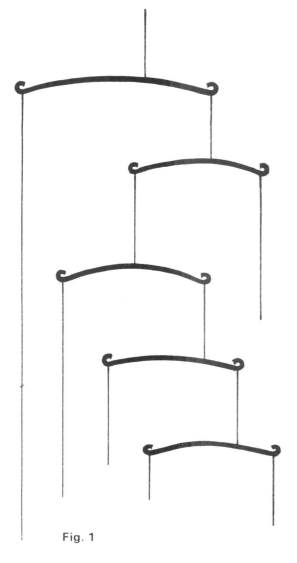

Fig. 1

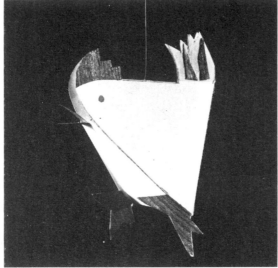

Beneath the chicken you see what is perhaps the simplest bird shape that you can construct from a strip of paper. Choose the colours carefully, and for all its simplicity, you will have a most attractive mobile.

The bird of paradise (pages 64 and 65) is especially beautiful—and far easier to make than you might think. If you carefully follow the instructions, and illustrations in fig. 3, you can construct it without much difficulty. For a bird of brilliant plumage, we suggest that you try working with the kind of gift-wrapping ribbon that sticks to itself when moistened. It comes in vivid colours, and even in stripes. As you experiment, you will discover many possibilities for colour combinations, and other ideas for materials that you might like to work with.

Step 1. Begin each wing by gluing four strips of paper $\frac{3}{8}$in (1cm) wide and $12\frac{3}{4}$in (30cm) long to another strip $1\frac{5}{8}$in (4cm) long.

Step 2. Weave both wings as follows: Fold the right-hand strip at right angles to itself, weave it under the second, over the third, and under the fourth strip. Then fold the second strip (which is now at the extreme right) in the same way, weaving it under the third and over the fourth strip. It is essential

that you weave both wings in the same direction, and not, as would appear logical, as mirror images of each other.

Step 3. Place the two wings alongside each other as shown in fig. 3c.

Step 4. Interweave the strips which are now overlapping, being careful that the weave remains in a continuous over-under pattern. In other words, never draw a strip over or under two crossing strips at once.

Step 5. Bring the long strips upward, and interweave them to form the bird's hollow body. See fig. 3e.

Step 6. Complete the bird by drawing four strips each through the two openings at front and back, marked with 'x' in figs. 3e and f. Glue the neck strips together, tie a knot to form the head, and trim the end to a point for a beak. Glue the tail strips together at the point of juncture with the body, and shred the long ends to form the tail feathers. If you are using the gift-wrapping ribbon suggested earlier, you need only moisten the ribbon slightly wherever you want a joint. Also, you will find that you need make only a small cut into the ribbon, and it will tear evenly, lengthwise, saving you the trouble of shredding long strips with the scissors.

The body of the little bird (page 66, top left) is formed of a single long strip which is formed into three rings, beginning with the smallest. The protruding end is cut into narrow strips to form the tail. The head is a separate ring. The whole bird is perched inside an oval—an egg—of another colour. This figure is most appropriate at Easter time.

The colourful bird shown on page 63 is easily made of strips of construction paper. Form three rings of different colours, allowing one end of the strip to protrude. In joining the rings as shown, have these ends jut out on alternate sides of the body. Cut the ends as finely as possible to form the tail feathers. A single small ring forms the head, and with the addition of crest, beak, and feet, your bright little bird is complete.

The ever-popular fish motif (page 67, bottom left) is shown made of strong, coloured cellophane. Cut two circles of equal size, and cut a narrow wedge (the same for both circles!) out of each.

Overlap these cut edges and glue in place, to make the body of the *fish* three-dimensional. Cut the fins in one piece (fig. 5) and attach to the body. Add sequins for the eyes. Remember that cellophane is transparent, so

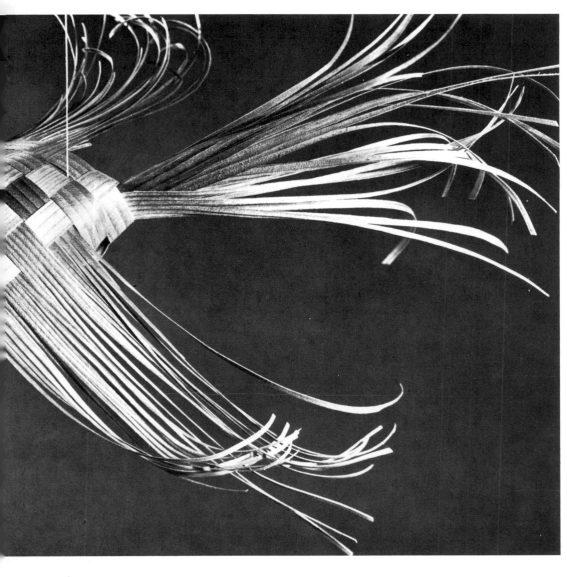

Fig. 2

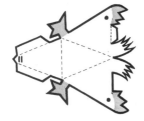

Fig. 3

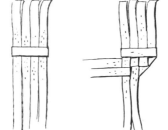

a   b

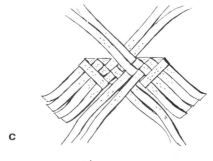

c

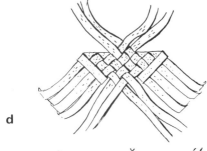

d

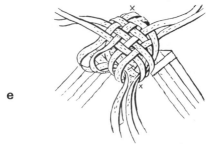

e

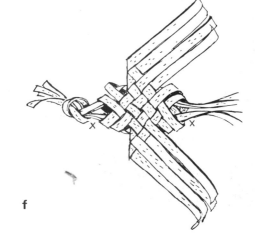

f

be very sparing in the use of glue.

Wood veneer is a beautiful, but very brittle material, which must be handled with great care. The fish shown on page 66, bottom right, is constructed in much the same way as the cellophane one. The fins are very simple in form, as the grain of the veneer is ornamental enough. The two long 'whiskers' of cane add a graceful touch. Finally, add two sequins for eyes. This fish is very appropriate for a man's room. It is very attractive all by itself, but of course you might wish to construct a mobile of several smaller ones.

The other fish on page 66, woven of strips of construction paper (or shining gift-wrapping ribbon: see the Bird of Paradise) is one of the most attractive figures you can use for a mobile. It is well worth your while to practice the somewhat more complicated weaving procedure until you produce a perfect result. Follow the diagrams in fig. 4.

Step 1. Take two strips of white and two strips of blue paper, each $\frac{3}{4}$in (2cm) wide and $13\frac{3}{4}$in (35cm) long. Make a fold in each, about $3\frac{1}{8}$in (8cm) from the end. Using two colours makes it easier to follow the instructions as given here. When you have become familiar with the procedure, you may use one or, if you like, four colours.

Step 2. Hook a white strip and a blue strip together at right angles, a short blue strip facing up on the left-hand, a short white strip facing down on the right.

Step 3. Interweave the other two strips, each alongside the strip of the same colour. So far you now have, from left to right: a short blue over a long blue strip, a long blue over a short blue strip, a short white over a long white strip, and a long white over a short white strip. If you have done this correctly, the reverse side should look the same as the front, but with the colours reversed (in other words, the square which forms the snout of the fish is blue on the side facing you, and white on the reverse).

At the points marked with an 'x' glue the upper strip to the one just below it. Do the same on the reverse side. Take care, however, not to join the front to the back by mistake. Now mark the ends of the long strips, a and b for the blue, c and d for the white. This again makes it easier for you to follow the instructions accurately.

Step 4. Bring blue strip a and white strip d together towards the middle, running them

Fig. 4

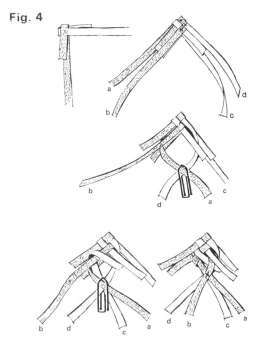

Fig. 5

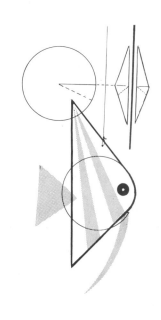

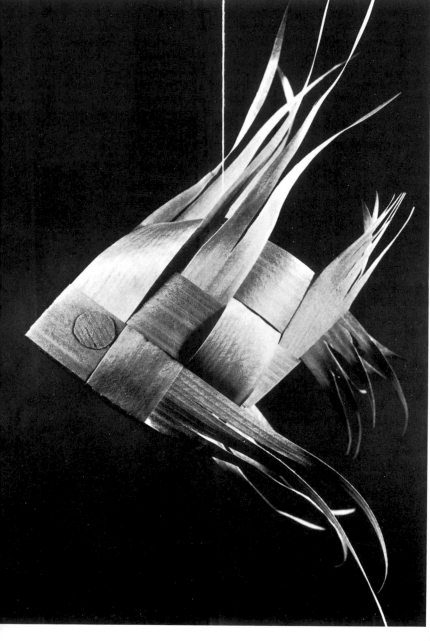

between the fins formed by the short strips; hold them together with a paper clip, making sure the blue strip is above the white one.

Step 5. White strip c is behind white strip d. Bring it up and weave it across the side facing you as follows: over white strip d, over blue strip b, under the short blue outside fin, under blue strip a, and under the short blue inside fin. Hold the end of strip c together with the ends of strips a and d, with the same paper clip.

Step 6. Turn the fish upside down, so that strip b comes to lie at the bottom right. Bring it up and across the top, weaving it over blue strip a, under white strip c (1), over white strip c (2), under the short white outside fin, under white strip d, under short white inside fin, and then over the white strip c (3).

Now hold the ends of all four strips between your left thumb and index finger, and pull on them gently by turns, until the body of the fish is smooth and slightly rounded. Place a drop of glue on strip c where the strips come together, and bring strip d up and over, pressing it down on the glue on strip c.

Turn the fish over again, place a drop of glue on both sides of strip b, bring strip a over it, and press all four ends together. The fins and the tail can now be trimmed on the diagonal, and fringed as shown in the photo. By drawing the ends gently across the blunt edge of your scissors, you can round them slightly, for a still more graceful and pleasing shape.

The hull and mast of this Viking ship are cut from thin cardboard and painted. The paper sails in a contrasting colour are attached individually.

The goose-girl in the centre column above will delight all children. Her head is a tiny red rubber ball with two thick braids of yellow wool. A circle of paper napkin is cut and gathered to form her skirt. The geese are constructed as follows: join a ping-pong ball (for the body) to a small paper or styrofoam ball (for the head) with a white pipe-cleaner neck. Add a beak of red pipe-cleaner pieces, and cover the body as shown in the photograph with real white feathers.

The roguish figures on the centre right, surely need not be explained in detail. We will just let you in on one secret: the hairpins of the impressive lady in the middle are nails covered with yarn!

The kites, top right, are an appropriate motif for a mobile. These are cut from construction paper, in carefully selected colours.

Another suitable shape for a mobile is a sphere put together with strips of construction paper, as shown in the photograph above.

At Christmas time, you might want to use gold or other metallic paper for an especially festive effect.

Decorations from Dried Flowers & Grasses

In one form or another, the fruits of nature are accessible to everyone.

Everybody likes flowers and most of us find them expensive. Not that that prevents us from buying them; there is no alternative. Or is there? What about dried flowers? Perhaps you've never thought of giving them to a friend. Or of making some dried-flower decorations for your own home. Or perhaps you've thought of it but lacked the stimulus to do anything about it. That's where this chapter comes in. Its object is to show you what can be done in this field.

Children are particularly good at the collecting game. Tell them what you want, and they'll bring back a mass of material which you can then get them to sift and arrange. That done, you can show them how to colour the dried flowers and grasses. At the same time, you will be teaching them in the most painless way quite a lot about botany.

Some of these decorations are ideal as table ornaments, others as Christmas tree decorations, and yet others as gay displays to hang from a ceiling or shelf. As always, the ideas that please you most will be your own.

Finally, when out in the country, remember to keep an eye open for likely materials: you may often find that each different area produces different specimens of the wide variety of flowers, grasses and colours that nature provides.

Our interest in making these delightful objects began when, walking in the late-autumn countryside, we noticed for the hundredth time how beautiful many of the dead and dying wild flowers looked. Our favourite in those early days was the hogweed. This was because of its impressive, open star-shaped structure. One day, we gathered a huge bunch to fill one of our big pedestal vases. We added to it a few sprays of thistle, tansy and yarrow.

The family was delighted. But it then occurred to us that beautiful though its shape was, the hogweed could be made much more attractive by the addition of just a little colour. So we picked out a particularly fine star and sprayed it lightly with a matt white paint. We also chose other plants of the same family (botanists call them umbel-

liferae) such as caraway and chervil and put them together so that a roughly spherical shape resulted.

Our interest was now thoroughly awakened. We saw that there were lots of things we could do with these natural materials, and so we started to experiment with combinations of grasses, flower stalks and seeds. Despite some failures, the results were on the whole very encouraging.

In the process of dyeing and drying, flowers lose their colour. But, like the hog-weed, they make beautiful shapes in dull grey or brown colours. Large plants, like teazles and bullrushes, often need no colour (though you may have noticed that people often do colour them gold or silver). But the smaller plants often benefit greatly from the addition of a little colour, or of a few highly-coloured artificial flowers. But this is essentially a question of individual taste. Only experiments, and perhaps the occasional failure, will show what shapes and colours go best together.

The results are nearly always beautiful and they are certainly a lot more impressive and satisfying than plastic or other types of artificial flower arrangements. They make splendid decorations for parties, birthdays and Christmas—especially when used to decorate the Christmas tree.

The suggestions in this chapter—and they are not supposed to be anything more than suggestions—are intended for all age groups, whether in the family, the school, the play centre or kindergarten.

Tools and Materials

The simplicity of this craft means that very few tools and extra materials are needed. For cutting the flower-cluster from the stem, a pair of pruning-shears is best. Use a quick-drying adhesive such as Bostik No. 1. Scissors, and needles in various sizes, will be needed, as well as an awl (or a knitting or darning needle) for boring holes. Twine or thread will be used for hanging the decorations but florist's wire may be used where yarn is likely to fray, as in the case of the brazil and hazel nut chain on page 73.

Plasticine is needed for decorations such as that on the bottom right. Brushes, tempera colours and bronzes will also be needed.

STARS WITH A CONE CENTRE

A pine- or larch-cone provides the hub of the star, and the grasses or flower-stalks are glued with Bostik No. 1 to the scales of the cone (after it has been allowed to open overnight in a warm room). Finally, the star may be bronzed or otherwise coloured, in order to stand out against whatever background you have in mind. In the case of the bushier pine, stronger colours must be used, while the fine-limbed silver-fir provides the best background for the more delicate grass and cone star decora-

tions. It goes without saying that the use of tinsel and Angels' Hair will spoil the effect of these natural decorations.

It would take an experienced botanist to recognize some of the plants by name, especially in their withered state, but all one needs in practice is an eye for what can best be used to make decorations of this kind.

STAR-BLOSSOMS

These are made from a combination of pine-cone scales and fir- or pine-needles. The scales are cut from the cone with pruning shears. The pine-needles are glued in a circle on a half-inch cardboard disc, to which the twine or thread for hanging is attached at the same time. A second cardboard disc is covered with Bostik No. 1 and attached so that the twine and pine-needles are firmly held between the two discs. After drying, cone-scales are glued to both sides of the disc. The finishing touch may be supplied by placing a small larch-cone or pine-cone tip at the centre. With these ideas as a guide, you can easily enough work out your own ideas. Many variations are possible with respect to size and materials, and a colourful centre can be provided by using bronzed thistles, artificial flowers, oat grains, small alder-cones and little acorn cups in a gay variety of combinations, on both disc-faces. The picture on the top left shows some of the possibilities.

VARIATIONS WITH SYCAMORE SEEDS

Children call these seeds by a variety of names and use them to make different patterns and to play a variety of games. Thrown up in the air they spin back to earth like helicopters. Our pattern is rather like a multi-blade propeller. The centre is a small cardboard disc. The seedbuds at the end of each blade are split and pointed, the two ends slotted over the cardboard disc, and then glued. The finishing touches can be added as illustrated on page 68, left. Alternatively, add whatever extra decorations appeal to you.

DECORATING WITH THISTLES

The picture, left, shows a range of thistles; some of them have been sprayed with bronze paint whereas others are as nature left them. An aerosol can allows you to spray on the bronze without mess or waste if you follow the directions carefully.

Two of the examples in the picture show how tiny artificial flowers may be used to good advantage, while another shows how the seeds of the ash may be coloured and glued to the thistle. The example in the upper right-hand corner of the picture shows how separate flower-stalks may be fixed to the thistle and coloured alternately in white and copper. The lower left example shows the effective use of silvered seedclusters

under a canopy of bronzed ash-seeds.

A host of other ideas will occur to you as you experiment with thistles as a base.

The illustration (page 68, right) shows a large thistle such as might grace the summit of a Christmas tree. A hole is bored through the head of the thistle, and its stalk is pushed through so as to protrude about three or four inches at the top and an inch or two at the bottom. A burr is stuck to the top of the stalk which is then coated with glue and covered with small artificial flowers. The upper stalk is then framed with a bow-like arrangement of delicate grass-stalks glued to the thistle at one end and to the burr at the top.

Use wire to fix the decoration to the tree.

ASH-TREE SEEDS

The decorations illustrated on page 69, top right, were the efforts of an eight-year-old girl, who used a quick-drying adhesive to fix the seeds. The decorations were then sprayed bronze. Be sure not to spray on the paint until the adhesive is properly dry.

Making dried flower arrangements stimulates a child's imagination, and therefore frequently proves to be an educational art as well as an enjoyable activity.

Pages 71, bottom and 72, top right, also show the fruits of a child's work. Ash-seeds and alder-flowers have been stuck to a pine-cone; cone and seeds have then been painted in various colours.

The basis of the most attractive decorations on page 69, bottom, is a ball of Plasticine. Soften the Plasticine in warm water, knead it thoroughly, and then roll it into a ball. Prick holes into it with a knitting needle and then stick the flowers in the holes.

Colouring should be done before the flowers are attached to the ball. In this way, the ball can safely keep its own colour which should present a pleasing contrast to the colours chosen for the flowers. The centre core could also be fashioned from wax or clay. If clay is used, then do not insert the flower stems until it has set quite hard.

The arrangements should be suspended on pieces of strong wire fixed to the centre core by forming one end into a small U-shape and burying it in the core, where they will set fast.

Plasticine can be moulded into a variety of shapes (disc, diamond, oval), providing attractive centres for a range of decorative forms. Carefully worked convex and concave surfaces can also be successful. The hanging thread can be attached to one of the flower-stalks.

The inspiration for the decorations at the top left of both pages 72 and 73, came from the hogweed. The star-shape is further enhanced by the addition of small, coloured pine- or larch-cones.

By adding flower-stems and grasses to the

open framework of the hogweed, attractive table decorations can also be made.

The decoration at the top of the picture on page 70 (top) shows the original effect of fixing a number of acorn-cups containing tiny artificial flowers into an open larch-cone. The hogweed brings out the over-all star-like quality of the decoration. The hogweed stems have been whitened, the artificial flowers stand out in orange, red or yellow, and the acorn-cups and the cone have been left in their natural colours.

At the bottom of the same picture, five white-painted thistle heads have been glued into a star-shape, with yarrow-stalks fixed between them. A beech-nut pod forms the hub, and artificial flowers are arranged in a circle around it. The hanging cord is attached to a point between two of the thistle heads.

The colour picture on page 71, top right, gives an alternative design. As in previous examples, yarrow-stalks are fixed between two cardboard discs. The inner star is formed of horse-oak leaves, the dark seeds of the pine-cone oat-grains. As the picture shows, an acorn forms the centre-point.

The illustration above shows two separate stars made of different ears of grain are

joined together between two cardboard discs whose surfaces are then decorated with artificial flowers.

The grass star (above) is formed by binding grasses together with thread and then gluing on maize-grains and artificial flowers. Oat-ears may be fixed between the grass-stalks.

Above right can be seen the effect of sticking sedge-arrows into the ends of grass-stalks tied together to form a star, at the centre of which maize-grains are glued together rosette-style.

STRINGS OF BEADS FOR CHRISTMAS (right)

These can be made from a variety of natural materials.

While still soft, maize-grains are threaded with twine. Short lengths of straw, maize-grains and fir-cone scales are strung alternately on thread.

Acorns and large juniper berries, while still soft, are strung together alternately.

Hazel nuts are first drilled through to take thin wire and then gilded.

Brazil nuts and hazel nuts are strung together alternately and then sprayed with bronze paint.

Puppets

If you're not yet ready to make a rag doll, why not try your hand at, or rather in, a puppet. Slip one on to your hand and these legless, comic-looking creatures will help you while away many a happy moment—with your own children or with friends of theirs who've come to tea. The shops supply a limited range of glove puppets but how much nicer to make them yourself. Then you will be able to give your children the puppet figures they like best. Or, even better, get the children to join in so that what results is their work, too. Children are especially good at sticking on weird-looking noses, droopy moustaches, and other such things. The older ones could help with the clothes. It's an amusing pastime and even quite a small degree of skill makes you independent of the shops and provides a use for the various bits of material most mothers put by 'just in case'.

PUNCH SEES THE LIGHT OF DAY

Creating the heads of these puppets will delight both young and old, for no shape or feature is so well known to us, or so variable, as the human face. We should not be too fussy or fearful in our first efforts. I once saw a photo that showed some blind people 'experiencing' a Henry Moore sculpture through their fingertips. We suggest that, while modelling, you shut your eyes from time to time and make a 'touch-test' as to the liveliness of the forms.

We study the faces of our fellow men to learn what particular facial expressions are characteristic of the various human emotions. It should not be too hard to transfer these characteristics to our puppet heads—in an exaggerated manner, to be sure. Don't be timid: a bold attempt is bound to meet with success. If we have started out to create a policeman, this does not necessarily mean that we will end up with one; a pair of wire-frame glasses will turn him into a strict-looking high-school teacher in the twinkle of an eye. The naming of what we make is in any case the last act of creation.

The Modelling Compound

Tear ordinary newspaper into 1in square pieces and soak them in hot water. Let them soak long enough for them to shred easily. Once the compound has been well ground up, squeeze it out well. (The compound can also be made from cardboard egg-cartons).

While the paper is soaking, prepare a thick paste, either made with cooked starch or bought in a stationery store. Mix a small amount of this paste into the compound, in order to obtain a modelling mixture which is not too wet and shapes easily.

A ready-mixed modelling compound is available in hobby shops.

Modelling with Paper Pulp

We build up the head around a cardboard tube of a size sufficient to admit the index finger up to the middle joint. (Make this from a piece of cardboard rolled into a tube and fastened with a strip of tape). The bottom end of this tube will serve as the throat of our puppet into which we insert the index finger when performing. A slight bulge at this lower end will serve to attach the puppet's dress later on. Once we have roughly shaped the head, we add chin, nose, mouth, eyes, and ears; as each of these is fashioned we paste over it pieces of white wrapping tissue (have a pile ready). As more and more tissue is pasted on, the form of the head should take shape and the surfaces become smooth. Forms that project rather far out, such as long noses, large ears, or horns, should be attached with the help of wooden pegs or matchsticks (see fig. 1c page 76). Dry the head in the open air, near a radiator, or at low temperature in the oven (leave the door open). After the model has started to dry we can add still more tissue to make the face even smoother if desired.

Modelling with Clay

Form a ball of excelsior (fine, soft wood shavings) the size of your fist around the neck-tube and wrap all round with thread. Fit this assembly into an inverted funnel to serve as a modelling stand. A bottle filled with sand, with a half-inch-thick peg stuck into its neck will also do (see fig. 1a and b). Now start covering the head with plastic clay. Start at the top of the head; use $\frac{1}{2}$in-thick chunks of clay about the size of a large coin, press them on well and knead the seams together. Cover the neck-tube also, and do not forget to add the slight bulge at the bottom. Now add the various features, re-inforcing where necessary with pegs, as above. The total height of the head should be about $3\frac{1}{2}$in to $4\frac{3}{4}$in. These heads should be dried at room temperature (in no case in the sun or in the oven)—this takes several

days. When the clay has hardened thoroughly, any unwanted or uneven areas can be sanded smooth.

Painting the Head

In order to be effective 'on stage', the head must have its 'make-up'. Use water colours, or even better opaque poster paints. For light skin tones use opaque white. A few colours well chosen are very effective at a distance. To protect the coloured head, spray on a thin coat of shellac.

Hair and Eyes

Wonderful coiffures can be made from bits of fur, wool, raffia, or tow. Braids may first be sewn with a sewing-machine to form a parting (see fig. 2a) Hair can also be attached in layers, working from the bottom up, much in the way a roof is tiled (fig. 2b). The eyes are painted on or represented by means of coloured beads.

Heads of Cloth

Cloth heads are attractive, but a bit more difficult to make (see page 74). Draw the profile of the head on cloth, and cut out two. The two pieces are joined by means of a strip of cloth running from the throat up over chin, mouth, nose and forehead, and over the back of the head to the neck (fig. 3). Sew these together to form the outer layer, which is stuffed from the

back with kapok. The ears are made the same way and attached to the head with needle and thread. The neck-tube should be made of soft leather in this case so that the dress can be sewn on to it. The illustration shows plainly how eyes, mouth and hair are made.

ANIMALS ARE INDISPENSABLE

The following instructions show how to make charming animals from cloth (various materials). Upper and lower jaws are cut out of cardboard (double as before) and covered with cloth. One of the upper cardboard jaw-pieces must be about 3in longer than the other pieces (fig. 4a, page 77). A sock filled with fine wood shavings is sewn on to this extension, shaped into the form of the head of the animal we wish to make (fig. 4b). The whole is now covered with an imaginatively patterned material which ends in a tube shape (fig. 4c). The inside of the mouth is covered with red felt, and a tongue of the same material is sewn in. If it's a four-legged creature, add two long ears of fur, a pair of paws, and a funny tail stiffened with wire. For a crocodile, teeth made from foam rubber can be nicely glued into the jaws. To make animals perform, slip fingers into the upper jaw, thumb into the lower.

Animals of Modelling Clay

Instructions for making a crocodile: cut out the basic shapes of the upper and lower jaws from a cardboard tube (see fig. 4d and e, page 77); the spots where the hinges go must be reinforced with cloth or thick paper glued on to avoid injury to the jaw while 'talking'. Upper and lower jaws are fitted with pockets (several layers of paper or cloth) for fingers and thumb (see fig. 4f). On to this cardboard frame we now shape the head using paper mixture or clay (fig. 4g). On the neck end of the head, leave an inch or so of cardboard, punch holes in it and attach the 'dress', a simple cloth tube wide enough to admit the hand and lower arm (fig. 4h). As hinges for the jaws, use two clips from manila envelopes. If you have metal shears, try using a tin can instead of the paper tube.

THE STAGE

The illustrations in fig. 5 show three ways of making a stage. If we want all the 'extras', we need model A. This is a stage that is placed on the table; it can be quickly set up and taken down. The two back wings serve as stabilizers and wings as well.

Model B is a practical, quickly improvised stage. A strong lathe is covered with felt at both ends and jammed in a door-frame. To this we attach a blanket to hide the performer.

Model C shows a very simple design especially well suited for children. A strong cardboard box is cut out as shown. The outside may be covered with gaily-coloured wall-

Fig. 1

Fig. 2

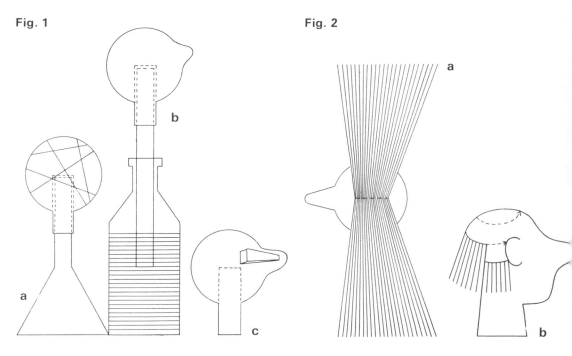

Fig. 3

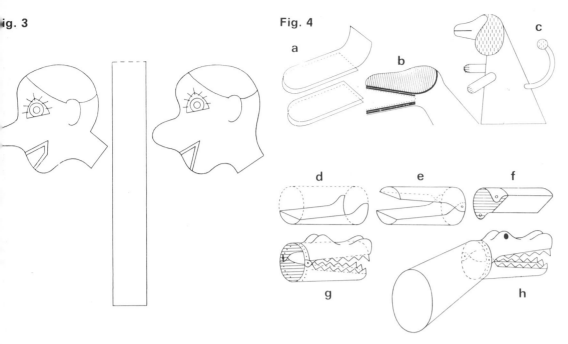

Fig. 4

paper. Use two tablecloth clamps to prevent the stage from upsetting while in use.

The Curtain

We must not underestimate the value of a colourful curtain for our stage. It creates the right atmosphere and serves to increase the excitement of the audience. The development of the play can be more easily regulated, and the performers can enjoy a few 'breaks' behind its protection. Here are two types of curtains:

A divided curtain which opens from the middle towards the sides, has small rings attached at the top and threaded over rods. The curtains are moved by strings pulled from the sides.

For a curtain that is raised and lowered, rings are attached to the material in three vertical lines. The draw strings run down the curtain through the rings, are attached at the bottom, and are threaded through three

Fig. 5

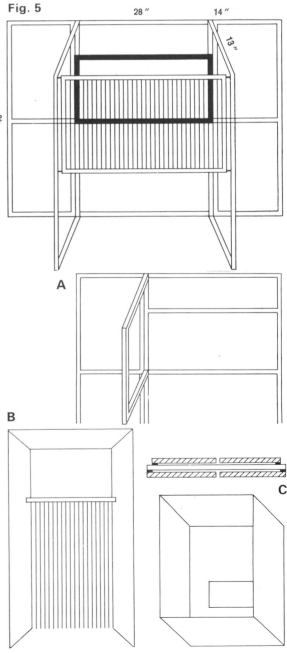

77

eyescrews on the curtain rail at the top. A strip of lead, or a quantity of coarse sand, must be sewn into the bottom hem so that the curtain falls by itself.

PUPPET COSTUMES

Costumes are also designed for effectiveness at a distance. Use brightly coloured material in contrasting colours. To this end collect not only gaudy pieces of material but also lacework, frills, veils, bits of fur, gold brocade, interesting buttons, feathers, tassels and fringes. The most attractive models in this chapter are completely improvised; nothing 'store-bought' was added. The basic costume is very simple to cut, as illustrated in fig. 6. The length of the costume is approximately 14in.

When cutting out this costume, take care to make the back part about 1–2in wider than the front. The opening at the top must be wide enough to admit the neck. The openings in the hands must fit thumb and middle finger. The hands are made from pieces of leather or felt and sewn together like mittens. The performer's fingers should slip easily into these little mittens. Legs can be ignored, as they are not necessary to the total effect. The finished costume is attached to the head over the bulge at the neck with twine (this allows change of clothes) or glued or tacked on.

Fig. 6

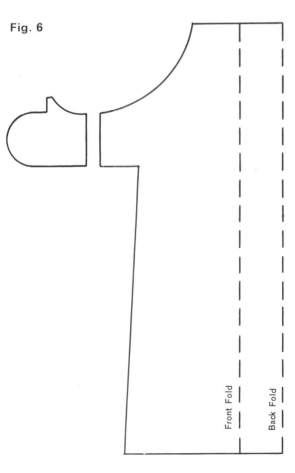

Front Fold

Back Fold

Homemade Enamel Jewelry

or this craft, you will not need a workshop. A fair-sized table (a card table, for example) will do very well. You will, however, need some special equipment. The most essential is a firing kiln, available in a variety of sizes and types. All the pieces illustrated in this chapter were fired in an inexpensive electric kiln with a metal hood, which does not consume too much electricity. You may add a larger heating surface and a hood of corresponding size. Since the various parts—heating coil and surface, and hood—can be bought separately, you can easily replace any of them. This small kiln is adequate for use at home, in craft groups, and in schools. However, if the kiln is to be used for the firing of small ceramic pieces as well, you will need a

somewhat more elaborate one, which is more expensive, and also consumes more electricity, since it requires a longer preheating period. Its advantage, of course, is that you can use it to fire larger enameled pieces, as well as small ceramic pieces. It is not worth while to build you own kiln.

Tools and equipment

You will also need the tools shown on page 80, top. The feeding rod is used to lift the metal hood from the kiln when firing is completed. The firing tray holds several small pieces for easier handling. The tongs are used for holding the metal pieces during the annealing (or tempering) process, and the slide for placing the enamel pieces on the kiln, and removing them after firing. The

kiln hood, and all other hot metal are placed on the asbestos pad until cool. For cutting the shapes which you are going to enamel, you will need two pairs of metal shears, for straight and for rounded edges. An awl and calipers are useful for transferring a design to the metal, but you can make do with an ordinary compass and a pencil. A wooden mallet is optional for flattening the metal pieces after annealing. For smoothing the rough edges of the metal and pieces, and for cleaning the edges of finished pieces, you will need a fine metal file (no. 2 grade). You will need a pair of flat-nosed and a pair of round-nosed pliers to form hinges and loops. A very fine nylon strainer will be useful for sifting enamel powder onto larger surfaces; small sifting tubes are also available. Finally, you will need fine steel wool, wine winegar, table salt, emery cloth, and water-colour brushes (no. 2 and no. 3 size).

What Metal to Use

For enamel-work, the best materials are sheet copper or sterling silver, which should not be thicker than $\frac{1}{32}$in. Brass is unsuitable, since its melting point is too close to that of the enamel powder.

The Enamel Powder

To enamel simply means to cover metal with coloured glass flux. We distinguish between several kinds of enamel. Opaque enamel completely covers and conceals the metal base. Transparent enamel allows the metal to show through. Opalescent enamel allows the metal to show through only after a second firing— but we do not deal with that type here. Chip enamel or mosaic enamel is produced by sprinkling a coarse enamel powder onto the metal base. The result is a somewhat raised surface.

Enamel colours cannot be mixed. They are bought ready to use. The red tones tend to be the most expensive. Transparent enamel powder must be 'washed' before use. To do this, place the powder in a clean bowl, add clear water to cover, and stir gently. Pour off the water with great care, to avoid losing any of the powder, and repeat the process until the water remains clear.

Clear plastic or glass tubes or jars are ideal for storing the dry powder. Mark the

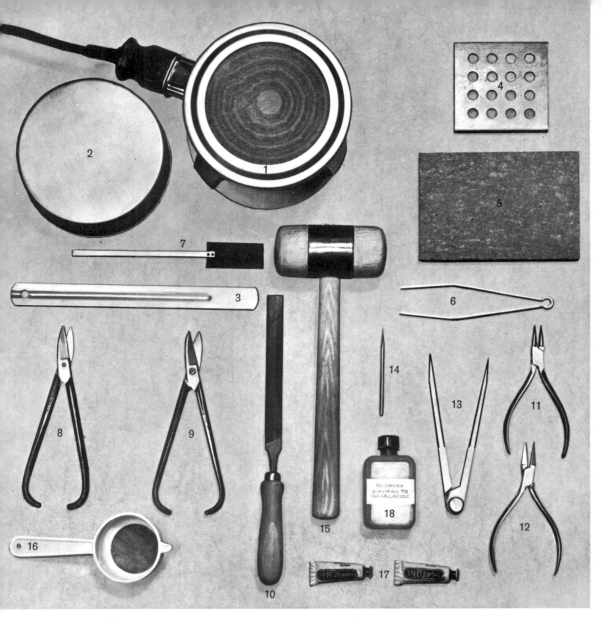

containers with colour and order number.
For best colour identification, attach a
small sample of the fired enamel.

Key to tools *(shown left)*
1. Kiln
2. Hood
3. Feeding rod
4. Firing tray
5. Asbestos sheet
6. Tongs
7. Slide
8. Metal shears (curved)
9. Metal shears (straight)
10. Metal file
11. Pliers (round-nosed)
12. Pliers (flat-nosed)
13. Calipers
14. Awl
15. Wooden mallet
16. Sieve for enamel powder
17. Metal adhesive
18. Tragacanth

Preparing the Metal

Copper sheeting must be tempered before
you begin to work with it. This makes the
metal less brittle and more pliable. Place the
sheet of copper on to the surface of the preheated kiln and cover with the hood, or hold
it with your tongs over a large, open gas
flame until it glows red-hot. Then throw it
immediately into a pan of cold water.
This will also remove the black scale that
formed during the heating. Dry the metal
carefully, and you are ready to begin.

Beginners tend to make the mistake of
being unduly ambitious. They often attempt
extravagant modernistic shapes, which turn
out to be rather disappointing. You will note
that all the pieces shown in the booklet
have a simple form, strictly geometric—
square, rectangular, round or oval—or
modified trapezoid or triangular shapes. You
will discover a wealth of variations of
these basically simple forms.

Sketch the outline on a piece of graph
paper, and transfer this sketch to the metal.

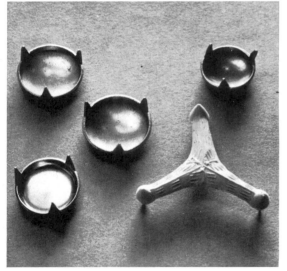
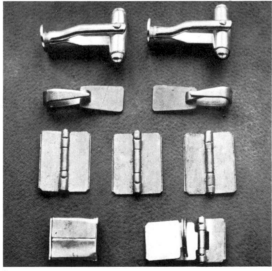

*Left: (from top to bottom) cufflink mechan-
isms; copper loops for pendants; hinges for
bracelets; spring lock for bracelets. Far left:
three-pronged furniture glider and ceramic
tripod for use in the contre-émail process.*

Fig. 1

Cross section of spring lock for bracelet.

Attachment for a pendant.

Fig. 2

llowing for as little scrap as possible. Cut he rough shape out with the straight hears, indicate the actual outline with your wl, and cut the final shape with the curved hears. If the metal is now bent out of shape, latten it carefully with the mallet on a hard, smooth surface. You may use an ordinary hammer, but in that case, you must protect the surface of the copper with a thin piece of cardboard, so that the strokes of he hammer do not show. File the rough cut edges and sharp corners. Now you must emper the metal once more. Then smooth he surface to be enameled with emery cloth, and rinse thoroughly with water. From this point on, do not touch the surface with your ingers, since any trace of dust or grease will keep the enamel from adhering properly. Finally, you must 'pickle the metal. Place it in a mixture of one cup wine vinegar and one tablespoon table salt. After a few minutes, remove it with a wooden tongs, or an improvised tongs of copper wire. Do not use tongs of any other metal under any circumstances! Rinse the metal and dry it thoroughly.

Applying the Enamel

Remember that extreme cleanliness is the rule from this point on, so clear your work tables of tools and other materials as far as possible of tools and other materials. Place the pieces of metal on a sheet of clean paper, and you are ready to apply the enamel.

In a small bowl (a clean fragment of glass will do fine for a 'palette') stir a small amount of enamel powder with enough water to make a thickish paste. (The beginner is advised to use opaque enamel, which is easier to work with). Apply the paste evenly to the metal with a water colour brush. The layer of enamel should be no thicker than half the thickness of the metal base, but the edges should be a little thicker than the rest. Place the pieces carefully on the preheated surface of the kiln to dry (use the slide for this). At this point, you may still smooth out any irregularities. When the enamel is dry, cover the kiln with the hood and switch it on. After a few minutes, lift the hood a little to check the progress of the firing. During the process, the enamel will discolour, but it reverts to its original colour upon cooling. When the metal glows red-hot and the glaze is smooth, it is time to switch off the kiln. With the slide, carefully lift the pieces on to the asbestos sheet to cool.

Now file the blackened edges, taking care always to work away from the enamel, as it splinters easily. Holding the piece face downward in your hand, smooth the back with fine steel wool or emery cloth, taking care not to apply too much pressure.

If you are enameling a somewhat larger surface, you may apply the powder to the metal base with a sieve. First coat the

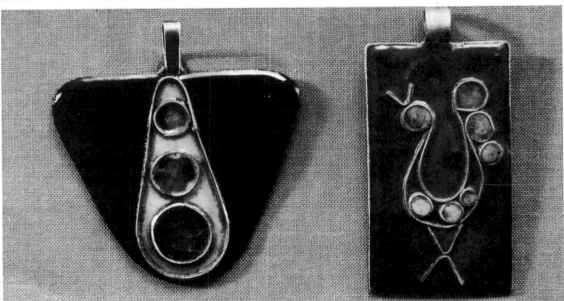

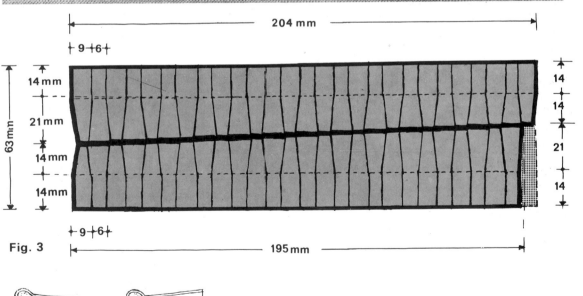

Fig. 3

Fig. 4

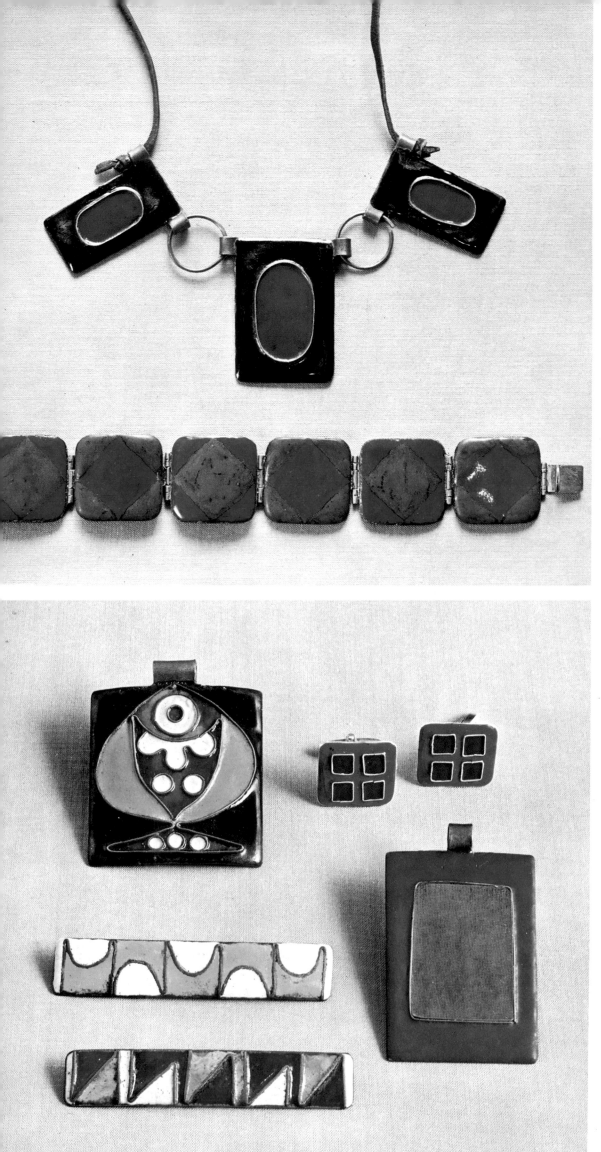

cleaned metal surface with a paste of tragacanth and water, and set it in a sheet of clean, dry paper. Now sift on the enamel powder evenly. Finally, raise the edges a little with the help of your brush. The drying and firing process remains the same.

To obtain a pattern, you may apply one or more colours over the first glaze. This second coat, however, must be even thinner than the first. For very small areas it is advisable to use a sifting tube. Repeat the drying and firing process.

When using transparent enamel, you must first fire on a colourless enamel. For the second firing, use transparent enamel in the colour or colours you wish. This technique is essential for obtaining the delightful transparent effect.

INSTRUCTIONS FOR MAKING JEWELRY:

Let us begin with a bracelet. It must be a little longer than the circumference of the wrist. You will find it much easier to gauge the size of each link (the links may be the same or unequal in width) if you first sketch the whole bracelet on a strip of graph paper of the proper length. Subtract $\frac{1}{4}$in from the overall length to allow for the springlock. Cut the links from a sheet of copper, and round off the corners a little with a file. After you have enameled the pieces, attach the hinges with metal adhesive to join them in an even line. The use of metal adhesive obviates the need for the rather complicated process of soldering. Take care that none of the adhesive gets into the hinge mechanism, and that the centre of each hinge is set exactly between two links. Clothes-pegs will hold the hinges in place until the adhesive is dry. Figure 1 shows exactly how the spring lock is to be attached.

The links of bracelet above are about 1in square. Since the hinges are exposed in this design, you must include them in your calculations for the overall length (count about $\frac{1}{8}$in per hinge).

The pendant on page 79, top left is cut from a rectangular piece of copper. At the centre of one of the narrow sides, leave a tab of metal $\frac{1}{2}$ to $\frac{3}{4}$in long, and no wider than $\frac{1}{2}$in (1cm) — see fig. 2. After tempering, hammer the rectangle into a slightly vaulted shape over a broomstick. Form the hanging loop by bending the tab forward at a right angle, and back.

The necklace on page 81 is made of five tongue-shaped pieces of copper alternating with six glass beads on a copper wire, not too fine, whose ends are formed into a hook-and-eye closure. The enamel pieces are $3\frac{1}{2}$in (7cm) long, $\frac{3}{4}$in (1.5cm) wide at the bottom, and $\frac{1}{4}$in (0.5cm) wide at the top. The loops are formed as shown in fig. 2 (remember that only the 'tongues', and not the loops, are enameled). If the wire is not 'springy', flatten it slightly by hammering it

on a smooth metal surface. The wire should not be finer than $\frac{1}{16}$in (1·5mm).

To make the necklace in the illustration above, cut a sheet of silver, $\frac{1}{32}$in (8mm) thick, and 8in (204mm) by $2\frac{1}{2}$in (63mm), into two equal halves, diagonally, fig. 3, page 81. Cut each half into small pieces, exactly as shown in the figure. Note that one piece of the second half is discarded (shaded area in sketch). Smooth all cut edges with the file and emery cloth. Shape the upper part of each little piece (the part having parallel sides) into a loop (see fig. 4, page 81, up to the point indicated by the dotted line.

After you have enameled the individual pieces, thread them on a silver chain, graduating the sizes from the shorter at the back to the longer at front centre, and alternating the two shapes—those which are wider at the tip with those which are narrower. The chain, which you can buy in a jewelry shop, or a handicrafts store which handles materials for jewelry making, should be about 16in (40cm) long, but may vary.

Contre-émail
When you are doing pieces in cell enamel, or are working with unusually thin, or large, copper pieces, it is usually necessary to enamel the back of the piece as well, other-

wise it will warp, and the enamel layer will be spoiled. Always enamel the underside first. You may use a mixture of left-over enamels. Only when the underside is finished should you go on to working on the front. Of course, you will not place the already enameled side directly onto the firing tray, since the enamel would melt and stick to the tray. To avoid this, set the piece onto a ceramic tripod or a three-pronged furniture glider (see photo, page 80). The marks which the tripod will leave are negligible.

Cell Enameling
In this process, the enamel is divided into areas of colour 'walled off' with shapes of copper or silver wire. You may use round wire, or square or rectangular. You may also flatten round wire with a mallet on a smooth metal surface.

First, temper the wire. (This is not necessary if the wire is very thin). Then bend it into the shapes you want. We have provided you with a good variety of designs you might want to try, but of course you will be eager to invent your own.

The wires must not overlap. Rectangular wire must rest on its narrow edge. The forms must lie smoothly on the piece to be enameled. 'Pickle' both the metal piece and the wire you will use. Sprinkle the surface

evenly with 'fondant' (a colourless enamel), and carefully set the wire forms in place with a pair of tweezers. Fire the two together. 'Pickle' the piece again. Now you may apply the various colours of enamel to the areas, bringing the enamel paste carefully up to the wire 'walls'. Do not apply the enamel too thickly. If you are already quite proficient in the enameling process, you may omit the treatment of the piece with 'fondant' when you use opaque colours. When the pieces are finished, carefully clean the wire edges with very fine steel wool.

Copper pendant on page 79, bottom right. Note that you must first bend the two tabs forward, so that you can cut away the strip between them.

Square cufflinks of sterling silver. The design is formed with small squares of silver wire. The mechanism of the cufflinks is also of sterling, attached with metal adhesive. (See colour photo on page 82, bottom.)

Two brooches with copper wire cells (colour picture, page 82, bottom). The cells, which are open, are not in one piece but formed of individual pieces, and put together to form the design.

For the triple pendant on page 82, three pieces of cell enameled copper are joined with a narrow leather strip to form a pendant. For an interesting variation, the loops are formed at the side rather than the top.

The loops of the pendants on page 81 are in one case part of the copper piece, and in the other case a separate (store-bought) loop attached with metal adhesive. For these more complicated cell forms, shape the wire according to your sketch, and then fit it snugly to the metal base.

Link bracelet (colour photo, page 79). After tempering, the individual links are gently rounded by hammering them over a broomstick. This makes the bracelet fit more smoothly on the wrist. The cells repeat the shapes of the links in inverted form.

What Went Wrong?
In concluding, we would like to point out the sources of some of the mistakes that many beginners are most likely to make. If blackened holes form on the enameled surface during baking, you did not apply the colour thickly and evenly enough, or you fired it too long and at too high a temperature. If you are using opaque enamels, you may reapply the colour, over the first layer, and refire the piece. If your finished piece has black edges, you fired it too long and at too high a temperature. You must file the edges down to the metal, clean the surface, and add more colour in those areas. If you have applied too much colour, the enameled surface may burst, and whole chips of enamel may fall away. This can also happen if you cool the article too quickly and too suddenly. You can repair this, too, by the addition of new colour and refiring.

Things to make from Odds and Ends

Nearly every household has piles of old clothes and scraps of material packed away in odd places, occasionally to be pulled out and inspected with a view to throwing them away and making space but more often just put back with the idea that they may come in handy one day. Generally, however, they are stored away in order to avoid waste or in sentimental memory of happy occasions in the past. This chapter is an account of how they may be put to use, and also give considerable pleasure to yourself and to others.

Imagination

If you are interested in simple crafts, you will soon see how these materials can be used to make a variety of gifts that your friends will appreciate not only for their general usefulness but even more for the imagination and effort that you will have put into making them. In this way, sewing becomes a pleasant pastime rather than a chore, and you will derive pleasure from the combination of skill and imagination which you will show in giving new life to discarded scraps of material.

Gifts for all Occasions

Such is the range of simple but useful items which you can put together out of bits of material that you can very quickly have a rich store of gifts ready for any occasion, including unexpected invitations and all those anniversaries you are as likely to forget as to remember. Many of them, such as laundry bags, napkins, face-cloths and work-bags, are very suitable as presents. And any woman would be happy to receive presents like oven-gloves, pin-cushions, needle-cases, cosmetic-bags or scarves, both for their usefulness and for the personal touch you have given them. Besides being easy to make they are quite inexpensive and therefore a good way of solving the economic problem of providing gifts for the circle of friends that seems to grow larger each year. In addition, it is one of the best ways for a person to learn how to perfect the art of sewing, as one can proceed with confidence in the knowledge that mistakes are not costly and easily corrected.

Equipment

The right kind of working conditions are important whether you are producing clothes and dresses or just using simple scraps of material in the way this chapter will describe. For the small items we have in mind, you will not need the wide range of equipment that one associates with a dressmaking establishment. But in order to avoid unnecessary problems, you should have the items listed below.

A large pair of scissors
A small pair of scissors
Tailor's chalk in three colours
Chalk-sharpener (or knife)
A ruler or square for drawing straight lines
A box of pins (to be used only for pins)
Long, medium needles for basting or tacking
Long or medium-length fine needles for hemming and stitching
Tape-measure
White thread
Silk thread in assorted colours
Thimble (if you use one)
Ironing board, with sleeve-board, if possible
Electric iron (preferably steam)
Piping, braid, cord, bows, pompons, artificial flowers, crests, attractive buttons, beads and sequins

HINTS FOR THE BEGINNER
Pinning and Tacking

Before stitching on a sewing-machine, the particular part of the material should be pinned and tacked (in some cases pinning alone is sufficient) in order to avoid the disappointment of crooked seams.

Using the Machine

The secret of good sewing is a perfectly regular seam, and although a sewing-machine is quite easy to use, it is as well to practise with short seams on small pieces of material before going on to more elaborate projects. Both pinning and tacking are important when stitching two or three pieces of material together so that they don't slip out of position when being run through the machine. Take care in pinning not to get the pins in the way of the machine-needle. With very light materials like chiffon, for example, or heavy materials like leather, which are difficult to put through the machine, cover with tissue-paper, on both sides if necessary, before stitching, and then tear off the paper afterwards.

Parallel seams need some care in stitching, and if they are close together the edge of the presser foot can be used as a guide. Those farther apart can be carefully chalk-marked first or sewn by use of a special attachment. In fact, it is as well to examine the machine, its extra attachments and the handbook for

instructions in carrying out a number of processes that will enhance the appearance of the finished item.

Neatening the Seams
There are various ways of doing this, as indeed you may already have learned: non-fraying materials may be neatened by overcasting; thinner, non-fraying fabrics may be turned under and run, both on the wrong side. For towelling, again on the wrong side, a blanket or herring bone stitch can be used. In some cases, you may decide to turn the seams to the right side and cover with tape (strap seam) or turn under and embroider.

Beginners tend to finish the sewing completely before ironing, and as a consequence they face a lot of problems. The more experienced needlewoman does her ironing after completing each separate step and thus finds it easier to get the material into shape. If you don't have a steam-iron, you must use a damp cloth in order to avoid bringing up a shine on the fabric, and don't forget that the seams must be dampened before ironing if they are to lie flat. If you are not sure about how hot the iron should be and how damp the material, try your hand on a spare piece of the material first.

How to Work Foam-rubber
Normally this will have to be sewn by hand since it is almost impossible to machine-stitch except in combination with some suitable fabric. It can be joined edge to edge by overcasting, as in the case of the Coffee Cosy Covers described on page 92. If, however, the seam is to be a flat one, both pieces are placed next to each other and stitched alternately on the left and right from underneath, in order to hold the edges firmly joined together in the right position.

If it becomes necessary to machine-stitch foam-rubber, then both sides should first be covered with a light, smooth material, like taffeta, for example, and firmly tacked before running through the machine.

Foam-rubber should not be ironed if at all possible, because of the adverse effect on it of conditions that are simultaneously rather hot and damp. However, it is the most effective insulation for Coffee Cosy Covers and Oven-gloves.

FACE-CLOTH (picture, page 84)
Materials needed: Towelling 17 × 23cm (7 × 9⅖in); Flower pattern and 18 × 21cm (7⅖ × 8⅗in two tone); silk thread; material for loop. This can be made from towelling scraps to be found in any household, such as the ends of worn-out towels, and the pieces that remain from your dress-making efforts. Even the smallest pieces can be used as in the case of the two-tone face-cloth, upper left, and you will be pleasantly surprised to find how firmly the seams hold in the face of heavy, daily use.

To avoid excessive seam thickness, use

selvedges of the material as far as possible. In the case of the two-tone one, stitch both pieces together on the wrong side, fold and stitch side and bottom seams on the wrong side, turn right-side-out and finally stitch the upper seam once (twice if no selvedges), incorporating the loop in the seam at the same time. The loop can be made from tape, bias binding or even towelling.

OVEN-GLOVES (picture, page 85)
Materials needed for one pair: Fabric 35 × 80cm (14$\frac{1}{2}$ × 32$\frac{3}{5}$in); Lining 35 × 80cm; Foam-rubber 35 × 80cm; silk thread; cotton bias-binding 2·5cm (1in).

The gloves are not only useful in protecting your hands while handling hot saucepans and so on, but also gaily decorative if made from brightly coloured material.

Use good washable materials for both the outer glove and the lining, and to avoid shrinkage, soak well before cutting and sewing.

Foam-rubber provides the best insulation and is generally quite easily obtainable, although in case of difficulty shoulder-padding can be used.

If you have enough materials, your lining can be the same as the outer covering of the glove. If not, choose a colour for the lining that will match the gay outer covering.

Instructions: Place your hand on a piece of paper and draw generously around it, leaving a good curve between thumb and rest of the hand to make sewing easier.

Seamed Glove
Cut out according to the glove pattern as follows: four pieces of the outer material with an extra $\frac{1}{2}$cm ($\frac{1}{5}$in) for the seam and an extra 2cm ($\frac{4}{5}$in) for the hem; four pieces for the lining allowing 2 or 3cm ($\frac{4}{5}$ or 1$\frac{1}{5}$in) for the seam and 1cm ($\frac{2}{5}$in) for the hem; four pieces of foam-rubber exactly as drawn.

Then, except for the wrist-opening, of course, sew up the lining and outer materials so that you have two separate pairs of gloves, as it were. Clip the seam allowance to the stitching line, especially between thumb and index finger, so that the seams will stay flat after pressing. The foam-rubber is overcast edge to edge by hand. Then put all pieces together—the lining wrong side out—and tack.

Glove with Bias-binding Edge
Cut all pieces without seam allowance, place on top of each other, tack and stitch close to the edge, which is then covered with bias-binding as shown in the photograph, page 85, tacking and stitching one side first, then folding over and sewing the other side carefully by hand.

The hanging-loop of the glove is made from bias-binding, which is twice folded and stitched, and then attached to the glove at the same time as sewing the edging around the wrist-opening.

Because of the foam-rubber, the usual final pressing should be dispensed with.

SHOE STRETCHERS (above)
Materials needed: Strong material or felt 25 × 30cm (9$\frac{4}{5}$ × 11$\frac{4}{5}$in); padding; silk thread; 2 curtain-rings. You can choose from a wide range of materials, including felt which is obtainable in attractive colours, but avoid using thick materials or those with a weave that is likely to fray. You can use the usual kind of tailor's padding, kapok or foam-rubber chips for stuffing the stretcher. Instead of curtain-rings, you can make loops from the same material or from a piece of attractive ribbon, if you like.

First make a paper pattern suited to the shoe of the man or woman likely to be using the stretchers, and use it for cutting four pieces of material with small seam-allowances. Place two pieces together in each case, pin and sew, leaving the broad side open for turning and stuffing, however.

Cut the seam-allowances just up to the stitching, turn and fill properly with the aid of round-nose scissors or a pencil. Firm filling is essential if the stretcher is to do its job properly.

Carefully hand-stitch the open end to-gether and sew on the rings or loops. Finally, press the stretchers into shape and they are ready for use.

COTTON-WOOL OR COSMETIC BAG
Materials needed: Fabric 30 × 60cm (11$\frac{4}{5}$ × 23$\frac{3}{5}$in); stiffener 12 × 20cm (4$\frac{3}{4}$ × 7$\frac{4}{5}$in); plastic bag; ribbon; silk thread.

Although such a thing is not absolutely necessary, it is a pleasure to use a gaily covered cotton-wool bag as you will see decorating the wall of an otherwise austere bathroom in the photograph, page 85. With a specially made hole in the bottom, you can extract the cotton-wool without removing the bag from its hook every time you need some. (Naturally there is no hole in the bottom if the bag is intended to hold hair-curlers and cosmetic articles that would fall through it!)

Practically any material of medium thickness may be used, such as velvet cord, cotton print, linen or towelling which are all hard-wearing and attractive. As a waterproof lining, use a plastic bag, and strengthen the base with calico.

The outer material and a piece of plastic, both 26 × 32cm (10$\frac{1}{5}$ × 12$\frac{1}{2}$in) are stitched together along one side and neatened by overcasting or turning under and running, so

that the fibres won't shred and get mixed up with the cotton-wool.

Along the other side, fold under and run a hem 2cm ($\frac{4}{5}$in) wide for the cord for which the inside openings are neatened with button-hole stitch. Use a double cord each one made from bias-binding with a narrow hem along each edge, folded and pressed before stitching. For neatness the ends are slip-stitched by hand.

In order to get a symmetrically round or oval base, fold the material twice over and cut out very carefully so that there will be no difference in size between the base and the material you have already stitched. If you are in any way uncertain about it, cut out a paper pattern first.

The base consists of three layers, the outer material, the stiffener and the plastic, carefully tacked together. Place a small piece of material right side up on the right side of the material, mark a circle about the size of a large coin and stitch along the line before cutting just inside the seam. Clip, draw in the seam-allowance, and neaten on the wrong side.

Finally, carefully join the sides to the base with fine stitching and neaten in the usual way.

PICTURE FRAMES *(left)*

Materials needed: Felt for back and front of frame; stiffener; silk thread; cardboard; adhesive.

Such frames are easily and quickly made, and with just a little extra thought and effort, they can be attractively decorated in the way illustrated on the left. Such frames add a rather personal touch to the photographs you may want to present to friends or relations.

Use the rather thick felt so that the frames will keep their shape. A stiffener is used to reinforce the upper side as well as the cut-out surround. While iron-stiffener is better, normal stiffener is fine if, in addition to stitching to the felt, you stitch close to the edge of the cut-out as well.

Use a fairly stiff cardboard, cut to the size and shape of the frame, and insert in the fabric as the last step in making the frame.

Cut the felt according to the size of the photograph to be mounted. You can get some idea of the correct proportions from the frames illustrated.

Carefully press the stiffener on the wrong side of the upper layer of felt, bearing in mind that this must be done dry to avoid spoiling the shape of the felt. If you do spoil it, a steam-iron must be used to correct it, but even that will only be partially successful.

Mark out the edges with a ruler and cut. Similarly measure and mark the cut-out for the photograph on the stiffener and cut carefully along the lines.

The first step is to run a narrow hem along the upper edge of the front layer of felt alone.

This is merely to match the rest of the hemming when front and back layers of felt are stitched together, because the top edge remains open to take the cardboard. Add the ornamental touches to the front, and then stitch back and front together along the bottom and both sides.

Remember that ironing has to be done dry and with a great deal of care. In the case of decorative additions which are difficult to hem, like those on the frames top right and bottom left of the picture, use a special fixative on them but cover the rest of the frame with a scrap of material before pressing with a steam-iron.

Cut a piece of cardboard to the size of the finished frame and slightly round the corners to make it easier to insert. It serves both to stiffen the frame and for mounting the photograph with adhesive to keep it in position. The photograph can easily be changed by cutting a new piece of cardboard and mounting in the same way. To hang the frame, a buttonhole-loop is carefully sewn to the back.

The top edge of the back flap of felt will have to be trimmed somewhat lower so that it will not pull above the front edge when hanging. Alternatively, however, the front and back edges can be carefully stitched over the cardboard so that there is nothing unsightly about the frame when hanging.

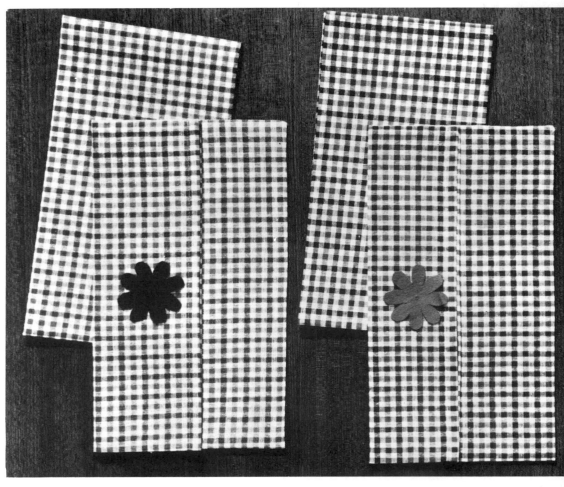

PIN CUSHIONS (picture, page 86)
Materials needed: Fabric 15 × 15cm (6 × 6in); padding; silk thread.

This is a small but useful gift appreciated equally by the woman who sews only occasionally as well as by the busy home-dressmaker.

Tiny pieces of fabric or felt can be used to make pin cushions that cost you very little in either money or time. The stuffing is just as easily available, and you can use ordinary padding, kapok, foam rubber chips or even foam rubber layers sewn together.

With a little thought, you will have no trouble in deciding what is best for your purpose.

Cut out two pieces of the material for the top and bottom, and stitch all round except for a small slit for turning and stuffing. So that the seams will lie flat, don't forget to notch the seam-allowances around the curves or to clip them in the angled corners.

Felt is non-fraying, of course, and can be fine-stitched in a simple seam.

Then stuff the cushion so that it is firm enough to maintain its shape and hold the pins and needles, and finally hand-stitch the slit to match the rest of the seam, inserting a loop for hanging before stitching, if so desired.

If you are not superstitious, you can decorate the cushion with a number of gaily-coloured glass-topped pins before presenting it as a gift.

TABLE NAPKIN AND NAPKIN CASE
Materials needed: Fabric 50 × 90cm (19$\frac{3}{5}$ × 36$\frac{3}{4}$in); small pieces of felt; silk thread.

At one time, elaborately embroidered napkins were all the rage but at the present time prevailing taste seems to favour simpler styles, illustrated above, which are easier to wash and press.

Thin cotton or fine linens are best for making napkins since the material should be easy to launder. Avoid large-patterned materials in a variety of colours but also make sure that the colours are not too dark.

Table Napkin
Cut from attractive cotton material to measure 50 × 50cm (19$\frac{1}{2}$ × 19$\frac{1}{2}$in), which is a very good size for a napkin. Make a narrow hem all around with the sewing-machine.

Napkin Case
The material is folded so as to leave a flap at one end. Stitch the sides of the pocket and carefully neaten the seams, with a double turned 1cm ($\frac{2}{5}$in) hem for added strength.

The flap is folded double and stitched. Being doubled in this way, it is more likely to keep its position without curling at the corners. The flap is decorated with a flower cut out of felt and fixed in position with a tiny press-stud so that it can be removed before washing. Coloured borders have a good effect, fine-stitched into place before joining the side seams.

Instead of a border or flower decoration,

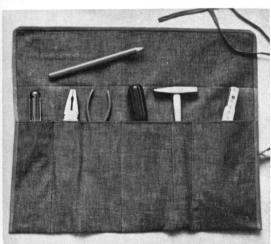

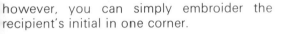

however, you can simply embroider the recipient's initial in one corner.

COVERED CONTAINER

Materials needed: Tin can, medium or large; fabric for covering and lining; silk thread; adhesive.

You can never have too many gaily covered containers of this kind, because of the thousand and one things that you need to keep safely and out of the way. Even an ugly vase can be given a new lease of life when placed inside the covered can where it can hold flowers without offending the eye.

The tin can on page 88 has a covering of satin but any thin material will do, and stretch materials like jersey are especially suitable. Naturally, your choice of material will depend on the purpose for which you intend the container to be used.

You will need a piece of material measuring twice the height of the can plus an extra 2cm ($\frac{3}{4}$in), by the length of the circumference plus an extra 2cm as well. In addition, you need inner and outer base covers, cut from the material using the can itself for marking around in chalk. In cutting out, allow $\frac{1}{2}$cm ($\frac{1}{5}$in) all around for the seam. If you don't have enough material, you can make the inside and outside from two different materials, so long as you join them in a straight seam first. The outer base cover can be made from a different material as well, if necessary.

Allow for the slight difference between the diameter of the upper and lower halves in stitching the seam, so that the material will fit properly both inside and outside the can. The next step is to sew on the disc of material you have cut for the inside base cover, joining together from the right side and testing to ensure a good fit. It should be snug enough to avoid pulling and distorting the pattern.

Press carefully before drawing over the can. Cut off the bottom edge of the outer cover to leave just a narrow border which is clipped and glued to the base. Finally, press the other cloth disc you have cut for the outer base cover, place it in position and fine stitch by hand.

Beginners may find it easier to use a piece of felt for the base, and to glue it into position rather than stitch it.

JEWEL CASE

Materials needed: Fabric 50 × 90cm (19$\frac{3}{4}$ × 35$\frac{1}{2}$in); silk thread.

A case of the kind illustrated on page 90 is extremely useful when travelling, since it takes so much less space than a jewel-box in one's case.

The materials that go with jewelry are rich in texture and soft and luxuriant to the touch, such as velvet and flannel for example, which can be stiffened, if necessary. Felt also is suitable, and it will be worked without seam-allowances.

Cut out a rectangular piece of material measuring 50 × 62cm (19$\frac{1}{4}$ × 24$\frac{1}{2}$in), fold to measure 50 × 31cm (19$\frac{3}{4}$ × 12$\frac{1}{4}$in), and, except for a small slit for turning, the three open sides of the folded material are stitched on the wrong side. Trim the seam-allowances at the corners, turn the right side out and stitch the slit together by hand. Press the seams.

Fold the lower edge over to make pockets 14cm (5$\frac{1}{2}$in) deep, marking the separate compartments with chalk in sizes to accommodate your particular assortment of jewelry, and then machine-stitch along the lines you have marked. The left-hand compartment is stitched at the top and then opened at the side to take a zipper, so that it can be used for small trinkets like rings. The binding cords are made from a strip of the same material 3cm (1$\frac{1}{5}$in) wide, pressed along the edges, laid double and stitched together. It is positioned as shown, either being fixed while stitching the right-hand pocket or carefully sewn in place as the last step of all.

So that all edges will lie flat, the upper half of the case is also stitched close to the edge and pressed carefully along with the rest of it. If it is velvet, only press where it is absolutely necessary, and then, so as not to spoil the pile, by laying the material pile side down on the bristles of a hard brush while pressing with a damp cloth on the wrong side.

TOOL CASE *(page 89)*

Materials needed: Fabric 40 × 105cm (15$\frac{3}{4}$ × 41$\frac{3}{4}$in); stiffener 45 × 55cm (17$\frac{3}{4}$ × 21$\frac{3}{4}$in); silk thread.

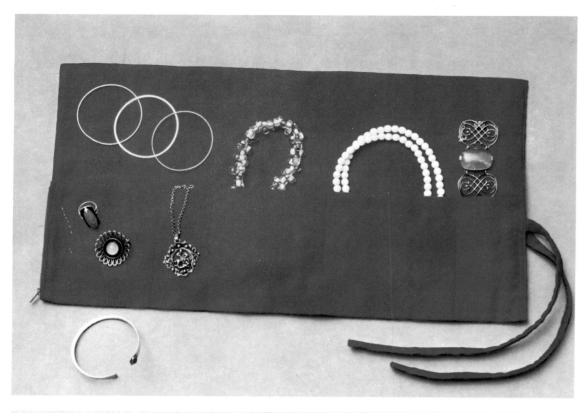

Similar in make-up to the jewel case but rather shorter, and wider from top to bottom in order to accommodate a variety of tools like screw-drivers and pincers.

Choose a sturdy, hard-wearing material which should be soaked in hot water before use to avoid subsequent shrinkage. Denim, sail-cloth, linen and all robust cottons are equally suitable.

Double the material (as you did for the jewel case) and press on the stiffener on the lower half of the material so that it has a certain firmness about it. Then fold over the lower part to make a pocket 19—20cm ($7\frac{1}{2}$– $7\frac{3}{4}$in) deep. Mark the separate compartments in chalk and run through machine.

Trim three sides of the case with cotton bias-binding in a matching colour. Machine stitch the right sides of the case and bias-binding together, turn the bias-binding over the seam and hem carefully into the stitches by hand. Slightly round the top corners first to make the addition of the bias-binding so much easier. The binding cord is made from about 1m ($39\frac{1}{3}$in) length of the same bias-binding, pressed, folded double and stitched along the length. Beginners may want to pin or tack before running through the machine. It can then be machine- or hand-stitched in place.

COVERED WALL-BOARD (page 90)

As well as being decorative for any wall, it also has a practical function in holding readily available in its pockets such things as scissors, keys and ball-point pens. In addition to providing a background for photographs, interesting recipes and newspaper cuttings, it also serves as an attractive place to mount things like stamps, theatre tickets, bills and other things that you will only remember by having them in front of your eyes in this way. It is a gift that will commend itself to a boy who wants to use it as a background for photographs of film-stars or sportsmen, while a business executive may appeciate its eye-catching qualities in drawing attention to important notes and sketches. For a young girl as well as the housewife and business-woman, it will be a welcome gift as well.

First of all, you will need a thin sheet of polystyrene measuring 50 × 70cm ($19\frac{3}{4}$ × $27\frac{1}{2}$in). Make sure that it is of a proper rectangular shape, trimming it with a saw or serrated knife if necessary.

For the covering you need a good, strong material which will not leave any pin-prick evidence of all the things you will want to pin in position. It is best to use one or two solid-coloured materials. Since you will want a rather restrained background for a somewhat bustling variety of things, you should avoid the added dazzle of patterned material.

The illustration on page 90 will give you an idea of the shape and position of the various pockets that you will want to add.

A few light chalk marks or full-size paper patterns can help you to do this. The pockets are folded back along the top edge pinned and tacked, and hemmed by machine or hand. All other edges are pressed and stitched about 1—2mm from the edge. In the case of the angled pockets, neaten as well to avoid fraying.

Spread the material over the sheet of polystyrene and pin at the back, making sure that it is taut over the front. Sew corners and use a smooth-faced adhesive tape around the border of the overlap to keep it firmly in position on the polystyrene sheet.

SCARF

Materials needed: Fabric 35cm (13¾in) wide and. about 1·20cm (¾in) long; silk thread.

Gaily coloured scarves go well with solid-coloured dresses or coats. It is best to cut them simply, rather shorter and narrower than one usually purchases, and to gain your effect by the addition of a coloured strip, simply placed as shown by the photograph on page 92, for example.

It is simple to make a scarf out of two, three or four colours, so long as the materials used are the same or at least very similar.

Naturally the most beautiful material for a scarf of this kind is pure silk but, because of all the seams, it should not be transparent. Twill is also good, but that is as strong a weave as you may use for this purpose. In addition, thin cottons, light woollens and artificial fabrics may be used with good effect.

The coloured strips of material may also be added diagonally or as lengthwise flashes, or indeed in any way that your own inspiration sees as original and striking.

After stitching in simple seams, press well as usual. The additional strips are made by doubling the material, right sides facing and stitching all around except for a small slit for turning. Then turn, press and carefully hand-stitch the slit.

LAMPSHADES

Materials needed: Lampshade frame; fabric measuring the circumference plus 4cm (1¾in) by height plus 6—10cm (2¾—4in).

The only kinds of materials for this are light, fairly transparent, washable materials since they are not only to be decorative but illuminating as well, and since they will gather dust from time to time, they should be capable of being laundered easily. The amount of illumination will be determined by the size of the lower opening as well, of course. Likewise, when you are buying the frame (and the other electrical fittings) consider the question of size and shape in relation to where you will be using it in the house.

Carefully measure the frame in order to ascertain how much material you will need. Allow 4cm (1½in) extra in the circumference and 6cm (2⅖in) in the length for the sphere-

shape (page 89) (about 10cm (4in) for the bell-shape, page 91).

Hem the material and neaten the seams. Very clear, transparent material should be lined with white cotton batiste, tacked into the seams of the material after neatening and pressing.

Sphere- and Cylinder-shaped Lampshades are covered in material which has a 2cm ($\frac{3}{4}$in) hem at the top and bottom, lightly folded and stitched in order to take a piece of elastic or cord.

Bell-shaped Lampshades are covered in material that is hemmed along the lower edge and given a broad turn over the upper part of the frame and hand-stitched inside to draw the material together around the throat of the bell-shape, as illustrated on page 91. Finally, tie a ribbon of the same material around the throat and fasten into a bow, both as added decoration and to hold the cover of the shade firmly in position.

For each type of frame, carefully stitch the material to the upper and lower parts of the frame.

TEA OR COFFEE COSY COVER

To avoid a merely homely, old-fashioned effect, give some thought in your design and choice of material to the cheerful effect that you want the cover to give.

You will need strong, washable material in cotton or linen, or some suitable synthetic fabric as well, taking the precaution, if necessary, of soaking it in hot water beforehand to prevent later shrinkage.

The foam-rubber insulation should not be too thin, of course. If you cannot get the right thickness, then sew two thinner pieces together, or otherwise use an equivalent layer of shoulder-padding. The insulating layer must be sewn against the lining so that it will keep its position between the lining and the covering material. If you use shoulder-padding, remember that you will not be able to wash the cosy cover yourself—it will have to be dry-cleaned.

Cotton braid makes a very good trimming since it is easy to work, especially on curves, and its definite, clean lines add to the functionally attractive appearance of the cosy cover.

LARGE TEA OR COFFEE COSY COVER *(page 89, background)*

Materials needed: Fabric, lining and foam-rubber, all measuring about 40 × 90cm (15$\frac{3}{4}$ × 35$\frac{1}{2}$in); cotton braid 1·15m (45in); silk thread.

Make sketch (fig. 1) full-size, and cut material double to match opposite sides. In the case of curves, fold twice into four layers so that you need cut only once for the sake of symmetry. Make allowances of 1cm ($\frac{1}{2}$in) for the seam and 2cm ($\frac{3}{4}$in) for the hem. Bear in mind the thickness of the insulating material, and cut the lining about 1–3cm

($\frac{1}{2}$–1in) shorter in the length accordingly.

Fold over and seam the covering material and the lining (separately of course), notch the seam allowances on the curves and press. Cut the foam-rubber exactly to size and over-sew by hand some distance from the edge to avoid later tearing.

Now place all the layers together, with the lining wrong side out of course, and tack all around about 4cm (1$\frac{1}{2}$in) above the lower edge. Turn the covering material up over the foam-rubber and stitch together. Then turn up and stitch the lining to the inner flap of the covering material. One or two stitches at the shoulder will suffice to keep the lining in position.

Finally, hand-sew the braid over the seams, as shown for example in the photograph on page 89. A loop of braid provides a neat grip in the middle of the top of the cosy cover. Remember to seam the ends by hand rather than the machine, and press flat for neatening. The finished cosy cover should preferably not be given a final pressing because of the effect of great heat on the foam-rubber insulation.

SMALL TEA OR COFFEE COSY COVER WITH SIDE-INSERT *(page 89, foreground)*

Materials needed: Fabric, lining, foam-rubber all measuring about 40 × 90cm (15$\frac{3}{4}$ × 35$\frac{1}{2}$in); cotton braid 1·15cm ($\frac{1}{2}$in); silk thread.

Cut out according to fig. 2, with a seam allowance of 1cm all around and a hem allowance of 2cm ($\frac{3}{4}$in) for the covering material, and $\frac{1}{2}$cm ($\frac{1}{5}$in) and 1cm ($\frac{2}{5}$in) respectively for the lining (no seam allowance, however, if the insulation is extra thick). The foam-rubber is cut exactly to size. The side insert is 8cm (3in) wide, with a length calculated from the position of the round shoulder.

With simple seams join front, back and sides together in the case of both the covering material and the lining. Machine-stitch again, notch the seam-allowances around the curves, and press flat together. To ensure that they will lie flat stitch from the right side close to the seam. The foam-rubber is joined edge to edge by over-sewing by hand.

Press covering material and lining before fitting together. Place all three layers in position, fold the outer cover under and stitch to the foam-rubber, then folding the lining and stitching to the inner overlap of the covering material. Sew on braid and bow by hand as the finishing touch.

FLAT-TOPPED COSY COVER FOR SMALL TEA OR COFFEE POT *(page 91)*

Materials needed: Fabric, lining, foam-rubber all measuring 25 × 90cm (9$\frac{3}{4}$ × 35$\frac{1}{2}$in); cotton braid, 1m (39$\frac{2}{5}$in); silk thread.

This cover is illustrated on page 91 and in the small sketch, fig. 3, on page 93. Cut according to the measurements of your offee pot, making the inner layers slightly maller because of their position. The size of ne lining will depend on the thickness of the oam-rubber insulation.

Join the separate pieces of the outer overing and of the lining in simple seams on ne machine, but oversew by hand in joining ne foam-rubber pieces edge to edge. The nside seams of the outer covering material re bound with cotton bias-binding in the usual way.

To ensure that the three layers do not shift ut of position, join the lining and the outer overing material to the foam-rubber insulation by sewing along the seam of the upper urve. Then notch the seam-allowances long the curves and press the outer material nd lining. Turn the outer material inwards nd up over the foam-rubber, stitch carefully nd then turn and hem the lining to it.

Finally, sew on the loop for the handle by and. You can use either the same material r doubled bias binding, but in each case, einforce with an inner layer of stiffener so hat the loop is permanently raised and easy o grip (fig. 4).

LAUNDRY BAG

Materials needed: Fabric 90 × 75 or 150cm 35¾ × 29½ or 59in); cord; silk thread.

Towelling is an excellent material for this ind of thing, although any kind of washable naterial is suitable. If the material is gaily atterned, then the bag can be made out of nat alone, instead of combining two colours s illustrated right, although that is by no neans difficult.

Lay your material double and cut out a ircle of 75cm (29½in) diameter. From the pper piece cut out an inner circle with a iameter of about 24cm (9⅗in), as illustrated n this page. Neaten the inside of the smaller ircle with a strip of towelling (or other naterial) left over from the piece out of vhich you have cut out the circles. Make wo slits in this strip and buttonhole-stitch or the insertion of the cord later.

In order to avoid the bother of constantly aking the bag off the hook and opening it n order to put something inside, you can nake a slit as illustrated in the photograph. t is about 15cm (6in) long and should be narked with basting thread before laying a iece of material, 20 × 8cm (8 × 3in), right ace up in the correct position so that the asting thread line is in the middle of it.

Then on the wrong side stitch around the asting thread as illustrated in fig. 6, with eams about 1·5cm (½in) apart. Then cut as llustrated, making sure that the diagonal cuts o right into the corners. Fold back and stitch, neatening the edges as well.

If you use two different colours and join hem together as shown, then take the maller circle you have cut out and sew to he bottom to enhance the decorative effect. f you have used pieces from the same pat-

Fig. 1

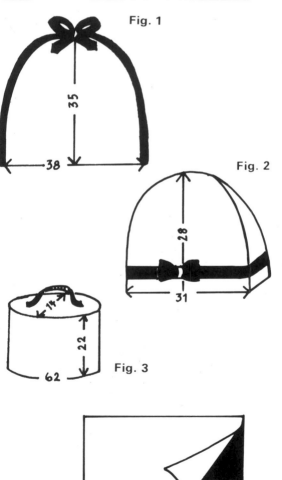

Fig. 2

Fig. 3

Fig. 4

terned material, then you can decorate by adding a tassle or a bow made from cotton braid, which material can also be used for the hanging cord and for covering the seams. Both circles are laid together with right sides facing and machine stitched before neatening in the usual way.

BREAD-BASKET COVER OR TABLE-MAT (picture, page 87, top)

Materials needed: for table-mat 50 × 40cm (19½ × 15¾in); border 1·2m (46¼in); for cover 40 × 30cm (15¾ × 11¾in); border 90cm (35½in) (or 35 × 25 and 85cm (13¾ × 33¼in) respectively); silk thread.

These are all easy to make, and they are particularly appropriate projects for beginners to start on.

Only good washable, rather stiff materials should be used. Linen is perhaps the best, although there are good cottons and artificial fabrics as well. Patterned materials may be used only if they are attractive on both sides, since either side may face upwards from time to time.

After cutting the material, measure 3—3·5cm (1¼–1½in) inwards from the outer edges and draw guiding lines parallel to the edges on all four sides.

Turn the material over to this line for hemming, pin and cut the corners with seam-allowance diagonally in the usual way. Then stitch the corners with the machine, making any alterations necessary to ensure that they lie quite flat when pressed.

Then turn the hem all around, drawing out the points of the four corners carefully with a needle before placing a gaily coloured border in position over the edge of the overlap and machine-stitching in place. The corners are notched rather than cut, and beginners will sew the corners by hand first, before tacking and machine-stitching.

Finally, both sides are pressed damp.

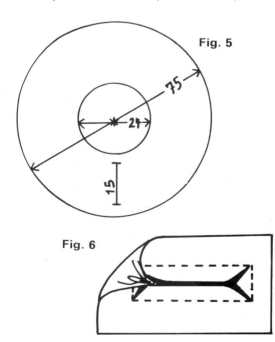

Fig. 5

Fig. 6

Clay Modelling

Clay modelling is an interesting and rewarding activity at every stage. The first touch of the clay brings back recollections of childhood, while moulding it seems to restore to us that sense of contact with nature, which our ancestors used to enjoy. Man and material join together in creative activity without the intervention of tools and machinery to stand between them.

Clay consists of tiny particles of worn-down rock washed away by running water to settle in the depths of lakes and seas, before being exposed once more, forming part of the land. There the clay waits to be used to build and decorate the homes of men. Firing at high temperatures makes the clay hard and durable. With this knowledge, pre-historic men produced a wide range of attractive and useful vessels but it was the invention of the pottery-wheel about five thousand years ago which brought symmetry and speed to the potter's craft.

The wheel is not as simple as it looks, however, and the beginner would do better to realise that using a potter's wheel is an art that may take years to master. You can, however, achieve early success in the field of coiling. In this, the beginner can acquire confidence and can exercise his imagination to the full. Indeed, many of the great modern potters produce many of their most striking pieces by this method, and the beginner might do well to emulate their use of the clay as a means of expressing their imagination and originality.

PREPARATION

Clay can be obtained from various sources such as brickworks, potteries, handycraft shops or specialist suppliers. Clay from the brickworks will need to be carefully sifted and sieved to eliminate any pebbles or stones. From potteries you should choose coarse- rather than fine-textured clay, since it is better for coiling. The fine clay feels like Plasticine, and it shrinks in drying and firing. Plates will rise at the rim in drying, but cracks will occur at the point where spout or handles have been added to a pot of particular design. It is easier to work with a coarser clay containing more sand.

The texture may vary, of course, according to the way you mix the clay. Generally speaking, however, the taller the pot the coarser should be the clay from which it is made. For the coiling process described here, it is better to use a fine red clay mixed in a proportion of four to one with quartz-sand. You should then add enough water to make a firm paste and this should be left to set for a few days and then spread out on a mortar-board to dry. Be sure first of all, however, that no specks of mortar are to be found on the board because firing will cause them to crumble out of the walls of the finished pot. Cardboard an ordinary wooden board or a stone slab will serve just as well for drying, and you will know that it has dried enough when you can stick your finger into it and bring it out clean.

In order to get rid of small air-bubbles that can burst in the clay during firing, the clay now has to be wedged by repeatedly cutting it in half and pounding the two pieces together again and again until you are satisfied (after about a dozen times) that it is ready for use. Two different kinds of clay can be mixed together in this way, using the wire (No. 1, fig. 1) for cutting the larger pieces, or thoroughly kneading the clay like dough.

To soften clay that has gone rather hard but which is still capable of being kneaded, mould it roughly into the shape of a cigar-box, bore a number of holes in one side (with your finger or dowel-rod) and fill with water. Next day it will be soft enough to work quite easily.

Clay that has dried out solid must be broken into small pieces with a hammer and wrapped in a wet cloth. To avoid having to take such steps, it is best to store the clay with a wet cloth over it in a covered plastic bucket. A plastic bag can be used to store

ny unused clay or unfinished pots and to
eep them moist and malleable.

ools and Aids

t first, while he is learning to mould with his
ands, the beginner will have no need of the
quipment shown below. Indeed, it should
nly be when the hands cannot themselves
o the job of shaping or decorating that other
ids should be sought. Most of those shown
n fig. 1 are available in most households,
nd the items numbered 9 and 11 can easily
e bought or even made at home. As the
eed arises in the text, the use of the following
ems is fully explained.

1. Cutting-wire	2. Plastic sheet
3. Wooden strips	4. Roller
5. Wire-strainer	6. Kitchen knife
7. Table-spoon	8. Sponge
9. Modelling tool	10. Brush (hair)
1. Shapers	

POTTERY WITHOUT A KILN

 would be a pity if you thought that pottery
/as something entirely dependent on a kiln.
 isn't, but that is not to say that we are going
 supply you with a revolutionary method of
ring in an oven or over live coals instead!
iring must be done in a kiln, of course, but
ere are a number of things you can make
/hich don't need to be fired at all. A good
xample can be seen in the solid-looking
andle-sticks shown above. Such designs
s these can be expected to last for years
efore firing. With this in mind, even with-
ut a kiln one can still get the thrill of
oing through all the steps from mixing the
lay to turning out an object of pleasing
hape and design. Since unfired clay is
orous, you cannot pour water directly into
 new vase unless you make it big enough to
ontain a small glass jar which will hold the
vater for the stems of fresh flowers. No such
recaution is necessary, of course, if you use
rtificial flowers or dried grasses. Instead of
lazing, you can use water-colours, over
/hich you later rub transparent (neutral)
hoepolish or beeswax to work up a gloss.

It is worth having a go at the candle-stick
esigns mentioned above. Before getting to
/ork with the clay, cover the table-top with a
heet of plastic so that you will neither dirty
e table nor find that your clay sticks to it.
hen take some clay and roll it between the
alms of the hands into a ball-shape. Drop it
n to the plastic sheet to flatten the base and
hen shape the sides and the top according
 the design you have chosen or worked out
or yourself. First however you should stick
e candle in the middle of the clay. To form
e grooves to catch the candle-grease as
hown by the examples middle and top left
bove, simply draw your finger lightly around
e central hole, always with the candle
tanding firmly in it. The bottom left of the
icture shows a more rounded design with

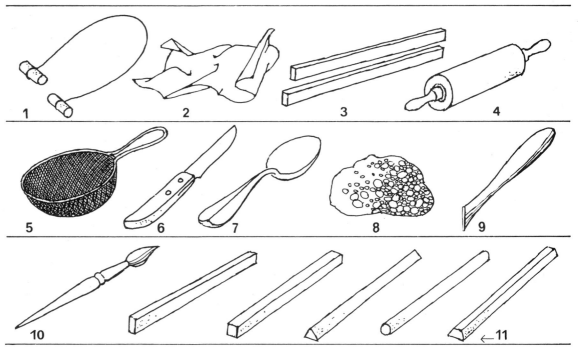

a coil added to form the neck. The examples also show how attractive patterns may be added by using pencils, rulers, paper-knives, bottle-tops and so on to make a chain of impressions around the candle-stick. In addition to the rounded design, conical and cylindrical shapes are also effective. These are made simply by rolling the clay out on the table with the hands and cutting off the length that is required.

FIRST STEPS IN COILING

It is better to start with something small and simple rather than to jump to the longer and more ambitious models that may have caught your eye as you have been leafing through the pages of this chapter. Be warned, however, that you will be far less disappointed with a clumsy little ash-tray than with the gross failure of a misshapen water-jug. For that reason, it is worth starting with the simple but attractive objects illustrated top right.

To make a small dish, first shape a ball of clay about the size of a tennis ball and then press it down into a disc about 1·5cm ($\frac{3}{5}$in) thick. You can either use the rim of a drinking-glass to press out the shape or simply use your fingers. To build up the sides of the dish, you use coils which should have been rolled out into lengths of between 30 and 40cm (12 and 15in). The left-hand, centre, photograph on this page shows you how to proceed by coiling carefully around the outer rim of the disc and pressing into position with the index-finger. As soon as you have wound a coil into position in this way, you should smooth the separate layers with the fingers both inside and outside, as shown in the second photograph of the pair. In this way you can either produce a cylindrical shape by carefully placing each successive winding of the coil immediately above the lower one or you can produce walls sloping outwards as you build up the coils with a slightly increased circumference at each winding.

In the same way you can produce the opposite effect by decreasing the circumference slightly with each winding. The example on this page (bottom) shows how this can be done.

The base need not always be round, of course, and you might want, after a little practice, to start building up your coils on an oval or round-cornered square base, for example.

The finished object should be left to dry for about fourteen days in a cool place, frequently turning it during this time to ensure balanced drying throughout.

Dishes, Vases, Jugs

On pages 97 and 99 you will see photographs of pottery with the coils smoothed on the inside only. In addition to saving time, this method gives the vessel a particularly sturdy and original appearance.

Although your first efforts are bound to be by trial and error you will soon begin to think in terms of modelling objects for a specific purpose. You will not only think about the use to which it is to be put, but its use will determine its size and proportions. You will consider, for example, whether the vase you want to make is to be used for a large bunch of wild flowers or just for a single rose. In any case, simplicity is the keynote of effective design and will show flowers to their best advantage.

Besides producing a firm base, you must ensure that the proportions of the vase are related to the nature of material itself; clay models demand a solid and strong appearance. Its very weight can cause problems, however. If, for example, you tried to make a soup plate at one go, you would find that leaving it to dry would cause the outer rim to collapse under its own weight. To avoid such a catastrophe, build up only a little at a time and allow each section to dry for an hour before an open window before adding the next coil. In each case, dampen and scratch the rim a little before adding to it, so that each additional coil will set properly.

While one doesn't expect the beginner's coiling to compete with the smooth appearance of pots thrown on the wheel, nevertheless a great improvement can be made by smoothing out irregularities. After drying for about a day, the pottery will be what is known as leather-hard and ready for gently cutting and shaving with an old knife or smoothing by tapping gently with a tablespoon. Sand-paper can be used for the final smoothing after the piece of pottery is dry. Such pieces would, however, have to be scrubbed with water to remove the dust which would otherwise prevent the glaze from 'taking' properly.

Even more care has to be given to the design of jugs where, for example, a small opening in the side would make pouring impossible without turning the jug upside-down! Likewise pouring can be made difficult if the spout is too small. The handle, too, has to be made strictly in proportion to the size of the jug and big enough for at least two fingers to get through it.

A technical point to note is that a simple but efficient spout can be made by placing the index-finger inside the finished neck of the jug, drawing it lightly outwards and at the same time pushing upwards with the thumb and middle-finger.

The handle is made from a coil or strip of clay that is tested out for the best shape and position on the jug, as shown on page 97 (top). It is fixed into position with the aid of a clay-paste or slip (clay in a liquid state) applied to the jug at both points where the handle will join it. The slip prevents the formation of air bubbles in the joints. Small lumps of clay are added and smoothed around the joints, both to strengthen the joint and en-

hance its appearance.

In order to avoid the danger of the handle's drying out more quickly than the rest of the jug and consequently pulling away because of shrinkage, the handle should be wrapped in plastic foil to balance the speed it dries at with that of the main body of the jug. It should be borne in mind that, as long as the jug is not fired, it should never be carried just by the handle.

Instructions for making the pitcher shown right are to be found below.

DESIGNING THE RIGHT SHAPE

As you grow in confidence and skill, you can turn to think about the question of design. One of the most effective methods is by drawing large-scale free-hand sketches with felt-pens on large sheets of wrapping paper. The outcome of your efforts is often surprisingly effective but in order not to leave things too much to chance, it will be as well to master first of all the basic shapes shown in numbers 1–5 in fig. 2.

Sketch 1 shows the simple austerity of the cylinder while Sketches 2 and 3, with their outward and inward sloping walls, are basically similar in design. Sketch 4 shows a design which has been popular from the earliest times because it has a special quality of combining volume and strength. Obvious variations of this design are to be seen in the egg- and pear-shaped designs which are still popular. Sketch 5, with its outward curving walls, is another basic popular design.

Naturally, each particular design can be varied according to the diameter and height as well as according to the slope and curvature of the sides. By combining the basic shapes, you can create even greater variety, as illustrated by Sketches 6 and 10, for example. Basic styles 1 and 5 combine to give you the design shown in Sketch 6. A combination of 2, 3 and 4 gives you the design illustrated in Sketch 7. Others you can work out for yourself. But you should remember that there is a lot more to it than merely combining a couple of basic ideas into a rather mechanical partnership. A lot of thought has to be given to proportion and contrast as well.

Pitcher and Mugs (above)

This is the kind of pottery produced to meet the needs of peasant communities in earlier times, to quench the thirst after hard work in the fields with apple-juice or tea. In your own household such a set will be both attractive and useful. In making the pitcher the main problem is that of making the spout. The walls of the pitcher are built up to the shoulders only and then smoothed inside and out. A hole is cut in the shoulder and the spout is made by coiling around it. You should pay careful attention to smoothing it, especially on the inside, before cutting off

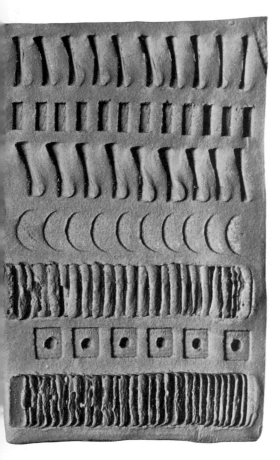

the end as shown. The neck, handle and lid follow. Instructions for making the latter are to be found on page 100.

Teapot with Cane Handle *(page 99)*
The inside of the pot and the underside of lid are glazed while the outside is left plain. The spout is made separately in a slap, bored through with a dowel-rod and joined to the pot with slip before carefully smoothing the join as shown. The lid is made by joining a flat disc and a half-round ball to provide the top grip, and a tongue is made on the bottom to keep it in place while pouring. Despite its striking appearance, there is a basic fault in this design, however, since it is obvious that the pot can never be made more than half-full. Ask yourself what simple change would have to be made to remedy this defect.

Vase with Chimney Complex *(page 98)*
This is the result of an experimental design aimed at producing an essentially symmetrical, multi-necked vase. The result is a rather austere, smoke-stack motif which lends both originality and power to a flower arrangement. A leafy branch is placed in the middle which blossoms from the same tree placed in the supporting funnels around it. The six short funnels are separately made, and considerable care must be exercised in setting

them over the holes made in the main body of the vase, since the joints can only be smoothed from the outside. However, an adequate amount of slip and a light smoothing are enough to ensure a successful firing. A striking feature of the design is the coiling of the lower portion to match the oval base.

For obvious reasons, it is difficult to create an entirely original shape in pottery, and while there is always the possibility of success, to try for it without the necessary discipline and insight is a guarantee of failure. On the other hand, it is a simple matter to incorporate one's own personal touch in pottery of traditional design. An original and attractive design can be made from the imprint of a door-key interspersed with raindrop marks made with the end of an ivory paper-knife. You can try out a variety of designs to be made in this way on a tablet of clay, as shown by the photograph on the left. You will find a variety of things, in a sewing-basket, writing desk or tool-box, for example, which, like the No. 11 shapes in fig. 1, can be used for stamping attractive patterns on your pottery. An even more original and personal pattern can be made with a stamp designed and cased in plaster. The pattern is cut out from the plaster with a sharp knife. Such stamping is best done on the flat strips of clay before they are

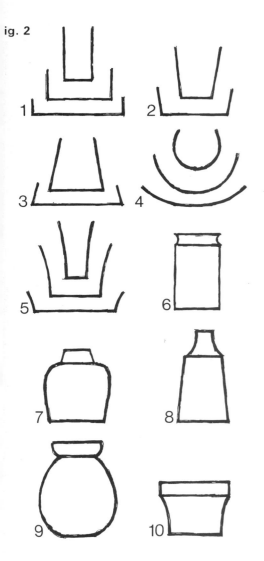

ig. 2

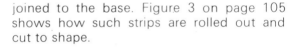

joined to the base. Figure 3 on page 105 shows how such strips are rolled out and cut to shape.

ENGOBE TECHNIQUES

Engobe originally meant the same as 'slip' which is the name for clay in a liquid state. It indicates the process by which a liquid-paste of clay, prepared in a particular way, can be used to add extra colour to pottery. In such a case, the pottery must not be fired nor should it be allowed to dry. It must be in that moist stage just before becoming leather-hard. In addition to pouring and dipping, the Engobe can be painted on with a brush (as shown above) or it can be applied with an eye-dropper.

In the case of blue circles on a white band, for example, it is important to allow the first coat to dry a little before adding the next colour.

Clays come in a variety of colours themselves, of course. In addition, Engobe can be purchased in the particular colours you want, and all you need to do is to add water and pass through a fine sieve. It is easy enough to make your own, however, simply by adding metal-oxides in the proportions shown below to, say, 100g (3oz) of white clay:

10% iron-oxide—red
5% cobalt-oxide—blue
8% brown-stone—grey
3% chromium-oxide—green
5% copper-oxide—green
10% Neapolitan Yellow—yellow
5% nickel-oxide—yellowish grey

The proportions can be varied very slightly, and the various Engobes can be further mixed with each other to give, with the self-coloured clays, a wide range of colour-possibilities.

The photographs above illustrate the way in which the basic character of the pottery can be enhanced by the addition of stripes in a variety of colours (top left), waves and dots (top right) a blue wedge-motif (bottom right).

Another technique, known as Sgraffito, is carried out by scratching out lines or small areas of the Engobe to reveal the colour of the original clay.

Ideally the texture of the Engobe should match that of the pottery to which it is applied, in order to avoid the possibility of peeling. Finally, you will find that a transparent glaze will further enhance the brilliance of the Engobe.

Candle-sticks

Using the Engobe-technique, the candle-sticks shown on page 101 were decorated in colours of blue, red, green and white. They are about 14cm (5$\frac{1}{4}$in) high, and, although they appear to be made of solid clay, they are actually hollow and made by coiling without a base. Such things as arms and ears can either be added in clay as shown below right or simply painted on as shown in the photograph. In addition to creating faces and bodies, you could decorate the candle-sticks in one colour only or with multi-coloured geometrical patterns.

Trinket Boxes

Any beginner can make the kind of pottery boxes shown on page 101, there is nothing very unusual about them except for the simple but effective designs impressed on the lids. Both are coiled although the one on the left can be made by the slab-technique described on page 105. In each case, however, the lid is made from clay rolled out as shown in fig. 3.

Although these lids are small enough not to require a knob, nevertheless an attractively-made knob can make all the difference to the overall appearance. Simply roll out a ball of clay and mould it gently into an original shape.

To keep the lid firmly in place, a smaller disc or coil of clay is attached with slip to the underside. Make sure, however, that the lid does not fit too tightly so that there is plenty of room for the later addition of a glaze on the inside. Allowances must be made for shrinkage as well, of course.

FIRING AND GLAZING

You need not be put off by the idea of firing because you don't own a kiln since it is fairly easy to come to some arrangement with a private pottery or with an educational institution. As you progress, however, you might want to co-operate with others having similar interests to buy a kiln or even get one for yourself. A wide range of kilns is available from such places as Art and Crafts Unlimited, 21 Macklin Street, London, W.C.1, and Sculpture House Inc, 38 East 30th Street, New York City.

The first (biscuit) firing is done, with a carefully loaded kiln, at a medium temperature of 850—900°C (1562—1652°F) which is reached gradually in order to ensure the removal of the water contained both physically and chemically in the clay. (Higher temperatures at this stage produce the red-brown finishes we know so well.) The kiln can be opened when the temperature has fallen to about 100°C (212°F).

Glazing is regarded as the climax of ceramic activity and while its primary purpose is water-proofing, the idea of decorating in rich colours is by no means just incidental. Glazes are available at reasonable prices from pottery-suppliers. You can get colourless glazes or matt and transparent coloured glazes.

Water is added to the glaze-powder to make a stiff paste which is then passed through a sieve before adding more water to give it the consistency of condensed milk. It may be kept in a tightly sealed and properly labelled plastic container. The first step in glazing the biscuit-ware—a vase for example—is to do the inside. Pour in small amounts of the glaze and gently rotate to ensure complete covering. Then pour the glaze back into its container, remembering to agitate it continually to prevent the heavier ingredients sinking to the bottom. Don't forget to mop up any spilt drops with a sponge.

There are various ways of glazing the outside, the most common being to hold the object somewhat tilted over the glaze container and to pour the glaze over it with a ladle. You will find that inevitably successive pourings overlap and produce deeper colours at these points. Experience will enable you to assess the effectiveness of such variations in the colour. (An example of it may be seen in the vase shown in the middle of the top picture on page 102.) A brush can be used to dab over those areas where the glaze has not taken, including one's fingerprints as well. Finally, glaze is removed from the base by sponging or, if necessary, scraping.

Dipping ensures a more even application of the glaze but for this you must have a container that is large enough.

Another excellent method of applying

glaze evenly is by using a spray-gun. Even the cheap little ones into which you blow can be useful as well. You must avoid applying too thick a mixture because it will tend to pull away from the top and gather at the bottom of the piece of pottery you have prepared for the second firing. You then have to file away the excess or remove it with an electrical high-speed abrasive disc.

You can experiment with the glaze to create different effects, of course. For example, the vase on the left of the photograph on the left has an irregular glaze applied around the upper rim and allowed to flow down freely as shown. An extra coat of glaze, rather thinner than the first, can be applied over a previous glaze to create an interesting effect. Again, different glazes can be mixed together before applying, and you will be quite surprised at the astonishing colours that will result. Or you may want to add a few extra flecks to the slightly hardened glaze to create the effect shown by the right hand vase in the photograph.

For glost (lead glaze) firing the pottery pieces are carefully packed on stilts so that they do not touch each other. The temperature is turned up immediately to 1000–1040°C (1832–1902°F). For various scientific reasons, hair-line cracks may be visible in the glaze after cooling, and the remedy is to wash out the inside of the pot with clear lacquer or hot beeswax to make it watertight.

Clay Toy-Town

You only have to watch small children for a short while to see how much fun they get from playing with clay, by pounding and rolling it, and cutting it into odd pieces with a knife. It is this kind of relaxed skill that can be utilised to make the mediaeval toy-town you see on the left.

The clay must be firm for this kind of modelling. Take the house in the middle for example—you can make it very simply by taking a lump of clay and knocking it against a flat surface until you have a clay-brick from which you can then cut away portions to form the sloping sides of the roof. Doors and windows can be made by adding small pieces of clay as shown in the photograph or by scratching the outline in the clay with a marker. Additions like chimneys, attic windows and steps are no problem as you will find out. The houses in the foreground, with an upper storey larger than the ground-floor is made by joining two bricks of firm clay together and then adding the roof and extras as shown. You will find that it is easier to model the solid structures or period-type houses rather than the indifferent lines of the *modern building*. While much of your toy-town will show the natural, untouched colour of the clay, you may, *if you wish*, add a little colour by using the Engobe-technique described already, to enliven the appearance.

Plaques

It is quite easy to cut out and decorate plaques like the one shown on the right and you will enjoy using your imagination to produce your own designs. Certain things, like cockerels, giraffes, turtles and sailboats are good in profile, while the best front views are of butterflies, owls, peacocks, crabs and lizards, blossoms and leaves, costumed figures and musical instruments. By making a small hole in the right place, you can mount your wall-plaque where it can be seen to the best advantage. You might even consider a series of figures to go with the surroundings such as a number of birds against the wall of the verandah or an 'Aquarium' against the wall of the bathroom.

If your clay is too fine, you will find that the plaques won't stay flat during drying and firing. It is better therefore to use a mixture containing 30–40% quartz-sand. Figure 3 on page 105 shows how to roll out the clay to the required thickness, making sure that you have a plastic sheet to prevent sticking, underneath. A thickness of 1cm ($\frac{1}{2}$in) is fine for plaques which are about the size of your hand.

First draw your design on paper and cut it out in order to use it as a guide for cutting out the clay with a knife. Smooth the outline of the clay afterwards, and then add such things as wings, fins and ears, fixing with slip in the usual way. Scratch in or stamp in the lines and the pattern you want, or just use the Engobe-technique which can be scraped to reveal the colour of the original clay beneath. Later perhaps, the Engobe could be covered with a transparent glaze. In making such plaques, you will quickly learn to adapt your design to the nature of the clay, and to avoid the thin, delicate appendages which so easily break off.

Cross (page 104)

As you look at the photograph of the clay cross on page 104, no doubt you will be struck by the way it suggests infinite possibilities of design.

The cross is 17cm ($6\frac{3}{4}$in) high and is intended as a wall plaque. It is, of course, still in its unfinished state. More work needs to be done to regularise the design before drying and firing, and finally filling in the separate cells with vivid splashes of coloured glaze or glass. (Look at the plaque shown on page 103 which has been finished in this way.) The mixture is one to one fine clay and quartz-sand, properly prepared before rolling out to a thickness of 2cm ($\frac{3}{4}$in) over which you lay your paper-outline before cutting the clay. You must not forget to make a hole in the back for hanging the cross. You can leave the surface smooth or form a pattern either by making shallow impressions in the surface or by adding strips or layers of clay in the usual way. The cross illustrated on page 104 has a pattern made by adding a

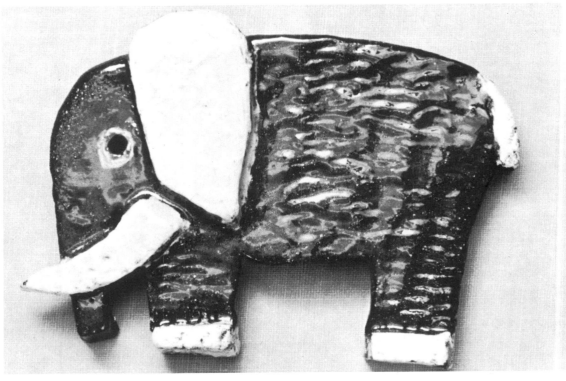

central disc and narrow strips to accentuate the plain geometrical lines of the cross. At the same time, notice the subtle effect of leaving out a strip (and thus creating three instead of four areas) at the top, with a matching omission at the foot, too. Whether you build up or gouge out is a matter both of taste and skill, of course, and again there is no end to the patterns that you can make around the edge, by means of the shapers shown in fig. 1.

Opaque or transparent glazes are used to fill the sunken areas of the biscuit-fired cross. Or you can colour by the Engobe-technique and fill up with transparent glaze after the first firing. Chips of glass from wine- or cosmetic-bottles may also be used (taking care when breaking them up, to do it in a heavy cloth, of course), and this is a further means of extending the range of available colours. They will fire at a temperature of about 1050°C (1922°F). An even more striking effect can be obtained by using small glass mosaics which fire at a temperature of 1000–1050°C (1832–1922°F).

CLAY CLOISONNE

As you can see from the colour picture (page 103), the pattern is built up by adding strips to a clay tablet. They are arranged in such a way that the plaque has a number of clearly distinct and separate areas (or 'cells' as in enameling) of various sizes which can be coloured with the glazes of glass chips described above. The wall-plaque can either be finished with a single glaze or gaily coloured as in the case of the plaque shown. In this case glass-mosaics were used for the cells while the strips were transparent-glazed.

The clay tablet is between one and one-and-a-half centimetres thick ($\frac{2}{5}$–$\frac{3}{5}$in) made out of the same mixture used to make the cross described above.

The tablet is surrounded by a solid-looking frame made from carefully cut, slightly dried strips of clay fixed in the usual way.

The pattern is transferred freehand to the tablet and scratched out with a modelling-tool. The shallow grooves are filled with the slip and overlaid with clay strips of a regular thickness (about 5mm–$\frac{1}{5}$in). The strips are smoothed on both sides with a modelling-tool. Two holes are made in the back of the plaque for hanging on the wall.

Since the strips are likely to shrink downwards a little, the cells or separate areas should not be filled with too much glass, in case of possible overflowing from one to another. This is a fault for which there is unfortunately no remedy once it has occurred.

A final word about possible designs for this kind of work—take another look at the suggestions on page 103.

Flower-boxes

The flower-box shown in the photo on page 105, right (with dimensions of 15 x 15 x 8cm—

6 x 6 x 3$\frac{1}{5}$in) can be glazed and used to hold one or more flower-pots, or left unglazed and filled with soil as shown. Such a box is particularly suited to setting off the exotic qualities of cactus plants, and smaller plant-boxes containing plants like these make attractive gifts for all occasions.

Figure 4 on page 105 illustrates the manner of rolling out the clay between two strips of wood. Note also the plastic sheet underneath to prevent the clay sticking to the table-top. The lower diagram shows how the slabs are cut with allowance being made for overlapping in cutting the end pair.

Since the slabs are rather long, it is advisable to use coarse clay to prevent shrinkage and distortion. The slabs are cut with the aid of a set-square or right-angled piece of cardboard after you have worked out the dimensions of the box you require. The slabs are left for about three or four hours to harden before joining them together with slip as described earlier in the text.

Plant-Pots of another kind

The left-hand photograph on page 105 shows how attractive and practical is a vertical arrangement of flower-pots, made with a solid

base as shown in diagram 1, fig. 3 and held in position on a long rod as shown in diagram 3.

It is best to make the pots all the same size and shape for any one set and to avoid crowding them together. The pots in the photograph have a diameter of 12cm ($4\frac{3}{4}$in) and a height of 7·5cm (3in). Using the same kind of clay and following the instructions given on page 104, roll out the clay to a thickness of 10mm ($\frac{1}{3}$in) for the base and 7mm ($\frac{1}{5}$in) for the side. You can use a conveniently sized dish or cardboard cut-out to mark out the base for cutting while a ruler will be needed to cut out the strip for the side of the pot. Allow them to dry slightly before joining together with slip as shown in diagram 1. Diagram 2 shows the arrangement for hanging the pot. The extra piece is moulded with the hands and a rod is used to bore a hole slightly larger than the length of rod on which the pots will be suspended, since there will be some shrinkage of the clay in drying and firing.

Diagram 3 illustrates the use of thick cord for holding the pots firmly in position. The cord does not pass through the hole at the side of the pot, of course, but is glued in position around the rod. Another method is to make a number of clay collars (diagram 4) and to use them between the pots.

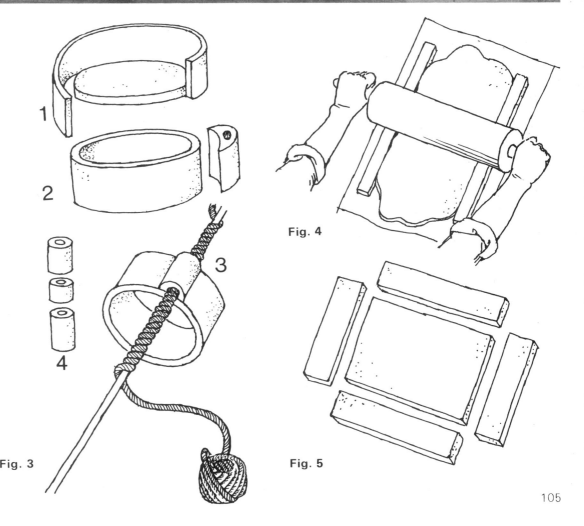

Fig. 3

Fig. 4

Fig. 5

Paper, Scissors and Paste

What better occupation for a rainy day than the creation of bright and useful objects with the help of scissors, paper, and paste—and a bit of imagination! Find a pair of scissors, big or small, sharp or blunt. Tear the brightly-coloured pages from old magazines. Supply yourself with a store of gay tissue paper, glazed paper, poster paper, drawing paper, from an art supply or handicrafts shop. Finally, make sure you have some paste on hand. Library paste is easy and economical to work with, or you might try rubber cement as is used in commercial art, or any of the great variety of adhesives suitable for working with paper. Lacking all of these, you may make a satisfactory paste with flour and a small amount of cold water stirred until very smooth.

The most appealing aspect of this craft is that you can create the loveliest objects, such as are shown in this chapter, very inexpensively and easily. The original objects can be found in great numbers in any household. Boxes of every size, tin cans with covers, glasses, empty containers and jars, small wooden boards, an incomplete set of building blocks—all these you can transform in any of the ways which this chapter will suggest and any of the ways which you will quickly begin to invent yourself.

There is no need to give formal and detailed instructions. Everyone is able to cut a piece of paper into interesting shapes, symbols, figures. It is rarely necessary to make a sketch beforehand, as the most original shapes are those which are cut freehand and without hesitation. When you have cut all the pieces you need, you are ready to paste them carefully on to whatever background you have chosen. Use extra care in pasting down tissue paper, as the colours may smudge. For small shapes, use a dot of paste at the centre; the edges may be pasted down later on.

Contact paper, obtainable in many solid colours, may also be used. It is best to cut out the shapes before peeling off the protective backing.

The colour plates in this chapter illustrate good use of colours. Remember that ill chosen colours or too great a variety of colours can produce a gaudy rather than gay effect. The examples shown in these pages are meant, of course, to stimulate your own imagination. Try not to follow them too closely, but let your fancy guide you as you see the paper taking shape under your scissors.

On this page and 111 are some examples in colour, of the objects you can create with paper, scissors and paste: a lampshade on a bottle, a waste-basket, around jewelry box and two gift boxes.

On page 110, we show two plaques for holding keys. Small wooden boards are painted with bright enamel. You may also use tempera or poster colours. After pasting on the paper shapes, add a coat of clear shellac for a high gloss and better durability. Add a few small metal hooks, and your key board is complete. Just in case you hadn't noticed: the polka dots, as well as the ringlet hair-do of the lady on the left, are easily produced with a paper punch.

The puppet on page 111 is so clearly illustrated that it hardly needs explanation. You can make it easily, especially after you have experimented with some of the other suggestions in this chapter.

It is far easier than you may think, to make truly charming packages for gifts. And not only will they delight the recipient, but their creation will provide you with many hours of pleasant activity.

You can make greeting cards and party invitation with a personal touch, using white notepaper or stiff paper cut and folded as you wish. Shapes are cut from brightly coloured glazed paper and stuck on. You will be able to think of many more designs as you work.

Page 107, top, shows elements of a very individual game of picture-lotto. Old magazines are a treasure trove for finding things to cut out and paste up—for example, the sunflower. Remember that you must have two of every picture for this game.

If you are making someone a present of a record, why not cover the jacket with your own design? Or you might present a half dozen embroidered handkerchiefs in a dainty box covered with tissue paper in two different colours, and trimmed with a lacy paper cut-out.

You can transform an old wooden plate into a charming wall plaque (page 108) by pasting on gaily coloured paper cut-outs. Everyone knows the technique of cutting out paper dolls from one accordion-pleated strip of paper. If you protect the finished surface with a coat or two of shellac, you may even use the plate to put food on when you have a party.

The calendar pictured on page 107 has captured the spirit of travel and adventure. Coloured tissue paper is the material used here. But be careful in your choice of colours. All too bright isn't always right. And do hang the calendar from two hooks, or it will gradually lose balance as the leaves are torn away.

A lampshade decorated with gay tissue paper fish is shown on page 106. The townscape shown on the wastebasket could also be used on the lampshade. Stylised flower motifs would also make a pleasing design. Heavy drawing paper is a good material for the background of a lampshade. Use tissue paper or very thin transparent paper for the design, so that the light can flow freely. Hardware and department stores carry the fixtures (usually on the end of a cork), for the lamp itself, and for the base, you will easily find bottles in a wide variety of attractive shapes and colours. For better stability, it is advisable to fill the bottle with fine sand before inserting the cork.

You can make delightful accessories for a children's party (page 108, top left) with inexpensive materials. For the place mats, cover a piece of cardboard with bright paper, and paste on whatever design you have chosen, for example, the group of frolicking children. The star-shaped flowers on the two glasses are cut from Contact paper, so the glasses may be carefully rinsed and re-used without losing their decoration. In fact, they are so attractive—and the glasses can be obtained so inexpensively—that the party guests might take them home as gifts. Table-mats are made in the same way as the place mats, and both are covered, for greater durability, with clear Contact paper. Place cards needn't carry only the name of each guest. Try adding a gay touch with cut-outs to harmonise with the other motifs you have chosen.

For a lovely Christmas scene, even the youngest in the family could help to cut out the simple, stylised figures of the holy family (page 110). Shepherds, and the wise men could be added at either side. Use heavy white drawing paper for the background, and tissue paper or glazed paper in vivid colours for the design. You may hang the finished

decoration against a window, or carefully crease a flap along one edge, so that it will stand up.

The picture blocks shown on page 109 can be rearranged to form many amusing combinations. The blocks are constructed of thin plywood, or of very stiff cardboard. In the first place, the sides are cemented together, in the second, use tape to join the edges. Then cover all the surfaces with strong paper of a medium or dark colour, and paste on the figures. The finished blocks should be protected with clear Contact paper or a double coat of shellac.

The small collapsible wastebasket (page 108) is constructed of separate cardboard pieces. Join the sides with tape (for greater durability, use a cloth tape, and burnish it down very carefully). Then cover the sides with coloured paper, folding the top edges to the inside to form a neat rim. Line the interior with glazed white paper. The bottom must be measured and cut very carefully, as it serves to keep the wastebasket open properly. The possibilities for decoration are endless.

On page 111, we have illustrated, in original size, a motif of yellow and red tissue paper, to give you an idea of the kind of design you might use to decorate gift boxes and other containers. It takes only a little imagination to develop an endless variety of ornamental figures or borders using geometric shapes and free-flowing forms. An *entire* surface could be covered with a similar repeat pattern.

You could, if necessary, buy an inexpensive wastebasket, but perhaps you have an old one at home which is no longer very pretty to look at. Cover the outside with heavy drawing paper (for the basket on page 106, we used an eggshell coloured paper), folding the upper edge to the inside, for a neat rim. Line the basket with strong paper in a solid colour (we used a brilliant green), and then paste on your design. Tissue paper is a good material to use here because you can obtain such rich colour varieties where the colours overlap. Our city on the river is, of course, but one suggestion. You might prefer a medieval townscape, with market place, aqueducts, water wells, and whatever else your fancy suggests.

Or you may decide to make a purely abstract design, with torn strips of black on a white background, or a simple chessboard pattern with some of the squares containing a small, amusing design.

When your wastebasket is finished, cover it entirely with clear Contact paper, to protect it from moisture and mishaps. You may wish, instead, to give it two coats of shellac.

On page 111, top, is another example, in its original size, of a repeat pattern of tissue paper shapes, this time geometric figures. Note how the three colours used—red, blue, and violet—produce a much greater variety of colours where the transparent surfaces overlap. A design such as this would make an effective border around a wastebasket covered with white or grey drawing paper.

For a box which might contain notepaper

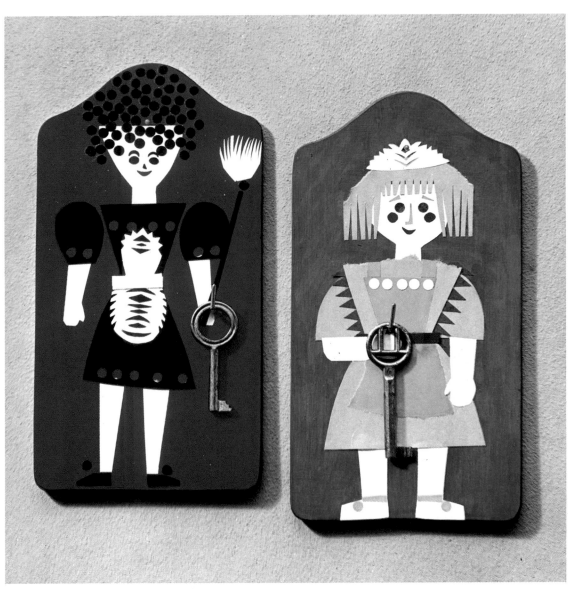

or a collection of small prints, you might choose a design of abstract forms used with restraint, so that the finished pattern is light and delicate. You might wish to add an extra touch of elegance by using a coarsely textured drawing paper in an off-white shade for the background.

In the photo on page 109, top right, are five more examples of the transformations you can bring about with the help of paper, scissors and paste, and a lively and free imagination. The box in the centre clearly indicates its specialised use for storing sewing things. The others might be used for jewelry, or as gift boxes.

Spice and herb jars (page 110) always make a welcome gift, particularly when they are accompanied by a rack which holds them. You can make a set like this yourself. Your kitchen will yield a good store of glass containers—small instant coffee, mayonnaise, baby-food jars, and the like. Paint the tops

with bright enamel. Cut the labels from light-coloured paper, and paste on the paper cut-outs. You may write the identifying names on the labels, or spell them out with cut-out letters. After pasting the labels onto the jars, be sure to give them several coats of clear shellac.

The round wooden box on page 106, which you can buy in handicraft stores, was given a double coat of bright enamel before the design was pasted on. Finally, the entire box was protected with a coat of clear shellac.

Old magazines will yield page upon page of bright colour that you may cut into the primitive shapes to trim place mats for a party. In the same way, you might make a wall-hanging for the nursery, perhaps using bits of felt or cloth along with the paper in making the design, and framing the design, under glass, like any picture, or pasting it to a rectangle of wood and protecting the surface with clear Contact paper.

Collage

Collage, which is simply the French word for pasting, is defined by the 'Oxford Companion to Art' as follows:—

'A pictorial technique by the cubist painters and used by Max Ernst and other surrealists from about 1920.

Photographs, news cuttings and all kinds of objects are arranged and pasted on the painting ground and often combined with painted passages.

In collage the objects are chosen for their value as symbols evoking certain associations whereas in *papier collé* the interest is rather in their form and texture.

A variation using pictures of parts of pictures is montage.'

The word collage refers to both the technique and the finished product.

The technique of collage, is to create a picture by means of securing with glue, any variety of shapes and objects to a board, to form either a pattern, a picture, or an abstract design of pleasing shapes. The shapes and patterns are endless. They include natural things like grasses, leaves, seeds and feathers; man made objects like bolts, nails, beer can tops.

As the background to the collage is often stuck on too, a complete co-ordination of design can be achieved by using a complimentary background to your design. The thin strips of wood often found in cigar boxes make ideal background to a modern metal collage, while hessians, felts, leather and other fabrics are ideal for more conventional design.

It has been found that collage is an ideal occupation for every age group. Very small children often produce amazing pictures quite quickly, and as many of the things used are household articles, it is an ideal entertainment for that rainy day. A ball of string and a tube of glue are a good starting point.

This art form is also an ideal therapy for those needing rehabilitation for a damaged limb. Recent results in a geriatric unit where patients recuperating from strokes were being taught to re-use paralysed limbs, responded wonderfully to making pasta collage where no cutting was necessary. So, we have an ideal hobby suitable for any age group, and either sex.

It is possible that the first collages were produced by primitive man to decorate hunting trophies such as shrunken heads and hunting shields. Rubber trees grew in tropical climates, and it seems possible that latex was already being used as an adhesive by peoples living in these areas. However, as little is known of this, and collage seems to have been neglected during the intervening years, one associates this particular art form with the present century.

Several of the French Impressionists used collage as an art form, finding the different textures of paper an exciting innovation. Picasso, too, was a great advocate of collage.

Each new art process in the history of art records events in time, and changes in technique, and collage is the ideal art form for this era. Never before have we had access to so many types of adhesive, fabrics, plastic containers, paints, enamels and aerosol sprays.

This in turn has made us look to nature for the natural forms of tree bark and dried leaves which no factory can emulate satisfactorily in plastic.

This chapter will, we hope, help you to look at things you see every day, in a new light. Examine the beautiful shapes of the metal tags we pull off beer cans; see how interesting strings of different thicknesses can be when draped together to follow the natural shape of an animal or bird.

Collect feathers, leaves, grasses and tree bark from a wood—discover how, when arranged on a board, these simple things can become primeval dragons, and feathered birds. Collect pebbles and shells from the beach. It is not necessary to *make* something definite out of them. Just admire their beautiful shape and form and colour; set them with

lue and keep them as a reminder of the implicity and beauty of natural form.

Collage must surely be the cheapest and most varied art form. Consider that almost everything you use will be a waste product of some form—newspaper, bottle-tops, nuts, olts, fabric scraps, broken beads—the list is endless. Apart from glue, a board on which o stick your collage, a pair of scissors or ome cutting implement, you need nothing more than a lot of rubbish and some imagination!

We hope that this chapter will re-introduce ou to many of the shapes which you regularly throw in your garbage bin. We hope it will encourage you to find other simple hapes and textures which you had never efore considered to be either beautiful or iseful, and we are sure you will enjoy inventing and creating a collage picture which will not only give you enormous fun, but, if idopted as a hobby by more people, could even reduce pollution!

The character of your picture will be dependent on your choice of subject matter and the availability of materials with which you carry out your design.

For instance, straw may suggest to you hatched roofs, birds nests, etc., while sea shells may conjure up beautiful under-water scenes, flower shapes or other such patterns.

The collage designs in this book are examples of the work of different people. They are not intended as patterns to be rigidly copied, but as suggestions for adapting existing bits and pieces which you may have n your own home. Explicit instructions have not been given with each individual collage because of the possible non-availability of materials but also, more important, your own imagination must play an essential part in this particular form of creativity.

BASIC REQUIREMENTS

Scissors (or cutting implement).

Glue: The following basic types should cover almost every requirement.

   (1) Rubber based: used for felts and fabrics.

   (2) PVA adhesive: for cards and papers (NB: PVA can be diluted with water.)

   (3) Transparent Plastic adhesive: for metal, strings, wires, fine things such as feathers, etc. (NB: big advantage it is transparent when dry.)

Boards: These can be stiff card, plywood, hardboard, the prepared types used by painters, or even rectangles cut from the sides of packing cases with shears or a sharp lino type knife.

Some Suggested Materials

Wools   Beer can tops
Pasta   Nails

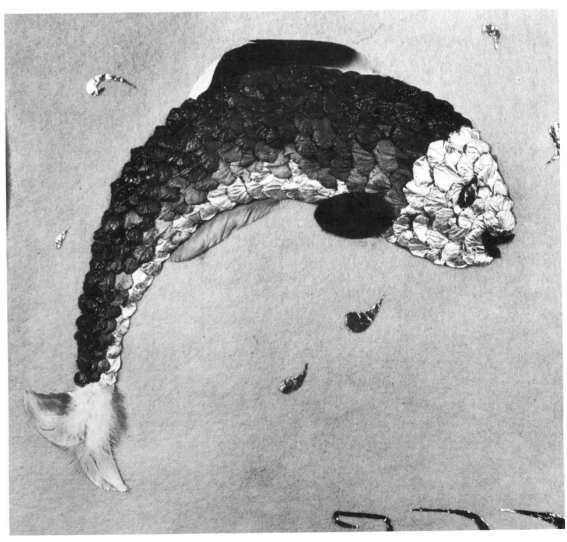

Scraps of fabric   Feathers
Nuts and bolts   Shells
Felt   Dried flowers and leaves
Straw   Twigs
Cane   Glass
Seeds   Drinking Straws
Buttons   String
Card   Newspapers and magazines
Beads

BULL *(page 114)*

String collage is one of the easiest and most attractive of all. String of different thickness should be used, and when curling string into circles between the fingers, it helps to hold it together with transparent or masking tape while it is being stuck. Do not remove the tape until the glue is dry.

Materials for making the bull: string, beads, board, card, hessian, glue. The bull was first drawn on card and the thickest string laid first round the head, chest and body. Thinner strings were used on legs, etc. Try to remember that although you are making a design from a natural animal, the form of the animal should be considered when filling in. When finished, cut carefully out of the card, spray with a bronze aerosol, and, when dry, stick down onto hessian covered board. (Coarse fabrics look better with string than velvets, etc.) Use transparent glue.

PIED PIPER *(page 119)*

This design was made entirely from scraps of fabric; the background of houses, and foreground area must be glued down first, and the figures stuck on last. Use a rubber based adhesive, and the most colourful fabrics you have for the figures, as these must predominate over the background.

BOATS *(page 116, centre)*

This collage is made from leathercloth. The shapes are simple, and leathercloth is easy to cut—there being no problem with fraying. Cover the board with background colour (most adhesives will be suitable) then arrange boats in a suitable composition. Put background houses in first, to allow the masts of the boats to overlap.

THE BOAT *(right)*

The boat is self explanatory. It consists of metal lids, curtain rail runners taken to pieces, knitting needles curved to shape the bottom of the boat. Tin tacks with wire threaded through, brackets, picture clips and small metal bottle tops.

The 3 ply wood background was first covered with fabric, and the parts stuck down with transparent glue. Always arrange your collage before beginning to glue, so that it is nicely placed on the background. Nothing looks worse than to finish a piece of work only to find it is lopsided. This is only one suggestion for a collage made from metal bits and pieces.

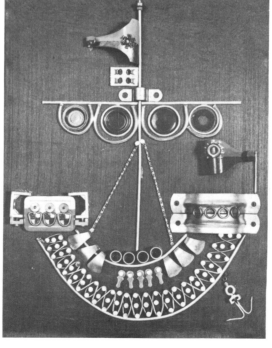

CASTLE *(page 115)*

Transparent collage. To make a transparent collage, it is essential to use a plain white background so that the colours can show through. This can be either a white board, or white fabric. Materials such as net, tarlatan, nylon organdie, etc., are used; each shape being superimposed over others, and glue with transparent glue.

STORKS *(page 112)*

The method for making the storks (page 112) is the same as for the lions (page 119). First cover the board using a rubber based glue, and keep the background soft in colour so that it does not detract from the design.

The trees forming the rest of the work are made from overlapping strips of felt using several tones of the same colour. The birds must be carefully drawn out. Stick the tail first, then gradually overlap *the* finely cut 'feathers' right up to the head. Beak, crest and eyes are added last. The larger 'feathers'

re nice solid shapes of felt and the fine
shaggy ones create the necessary contrast.

DRIED FLOWERS

The countryside itself is a veritable treasure
house of materials for the art of collage.
Dried flowers and grasses make charming
pictures, they can be bought cheaply,
gathered from the hedgerows or grown in
one's garden and dried at home. For a background, a piece of coarse woven fabric such
as wool, tweed or hessian can be used. This
is glued to two pieces of wooden dowelling
at the top and bottom, measuring approximately the width of the fabric, so that it
hangs like a scroll.

Using a transparent adhesive start by
glueing the smallest flowers and grasses to
the outside edge of the pattern. Retain the
largest flowers for the centre of the design
to give weight to the overall effect.

LION (page 113)

Made in the same way as the bull on page
114.

OWL (right)

Cork, wheat, 'honesty' leaves and other
natural things have been used to create this
charming owl.

A nice, coarse hessian type fabric was
used for the basic shape and overlapping
triangles of felts and assorted fabrics added,
creating the effect of wings. Using a rubber
based glue, start at the bottom of the wing,
and overlap the 'feathers'. Circles of 'honesty'
leaves, plaited wool or raffia) and felt, surround the eyes, and shells, buttons, or flat
backed beads make the eyes.

Start working from the outside of the eye,
and finish in the centre. Cork nose and feet
are added, and the chest can be textured
with a variety of things from small beads to
sycamore leaves.

The natural wheat and grasses (stuck with
transparent glue) soften the design.

FISH (page 113)

Cover board with either paper or fabric, and
cut a paper pattern for fish so that it is nicely
proportioned to the board. Begin by glueing
two feathers for the tail, and then overlay the
leaves like fish scales; the leaves can be
painted before-hand, or sprayed with silver
enamel. A combination of both is attractive.
Almost any paint is suitable for the leaves.
Add pigeon feathers for fins, and paint in an
eye, or add a bead. Use transparent glue.

PASTA (page 119, top)

Pasta can be bought in almost any shape or
pattern, is cheap, and easy to handle.

Use a piece of thick cardboard or hardboard for the background, then arrange the
pasta in any pattern of your choice, the
combinations are endless.

When you have arranged your pattern on

the board apply a little glue to the back of the pasta and stick down. Almost any glue is suitable for pasta. When dry, either spray with a metallic enamel, or paint any colour with almost any variety of paint.

DICKENSIAN STREET (*page 118, top*)
This quaint design is made from a combination of scraps of cloth. Cover the sky and background areas initially then add the houses. Use contrasting coloured fabrics from house to house, utilising braids, lace and tape, etc., to edge windows and doorways. Finally add the figures to create an

overall three dimensional effect. It is essential to use a transparent glue for the small parts and the narrow braids.

THE THREE KINGS (page 116)
This attractive 'Christmas' picture was made from a variety of coloured fabrics, bits of lace, wool, and pieces of non-tarnishable tinsel; all stuck onto a hessian background using transparent glue.

COCKEREL (page 116)
Cover a board with plain coloured felt or fabric using a rubber based glue. When dry, arrange feathers into cockerel shape, starting at the bottom so that the end of each feather is overlapped by the next. The outside wings should be arranged before the body is completely covered. Add felt comb, beak and feet, and a bead for the eye. Use transparent adhesive for feathers.

HYPODERMIC NEEDLE DESIGN
(page 116, top left)
This charming and interesting design was made from the throw away products of the medical profession. It is included for general interest only, as few of us other than doctors, nurses, etc., would have access to such materials. It is, however, a classical illustration of the art of collage by showing how such improbable materials can create a most artistic effect.

It cannot be impressed too much upon the reader that almost any waste product can be converted into interesting and exciting patterns.

CHICKEN (page 117)
A bent knitting needle made the outline and the rest were bits found in the tool box. Beer can tops were used for wings.

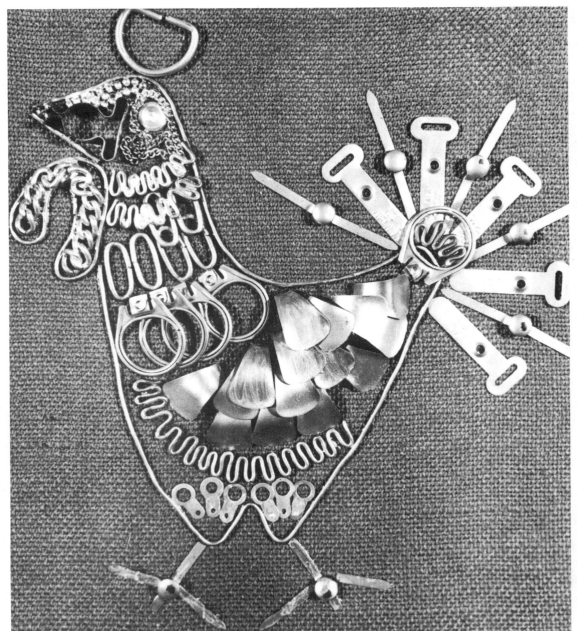

JEWISH TABLEAU
(page 118, bottom left)

This collage is based on a design carried out in modern form at an Israeli airport. It was based on an old testament figure, and is a mixture of different materials.

The design was drawn on to a large piece of hardboard, and the outline glued in with metallic cord. Shapes and patterns were then evolved in the design, making it fairly abstract. Tiles, string, pasta, metal rings and lentils were used to create the different patterns and textures, and then the whole thing was sprayed bronze.

When dry, patterns were picked out in enamels, and quite large areas filled in with colour, leaving bands of bronze showing.

AZTEC *(page 118, bottom right)*

Most of the parts for this Mayan figure were found by using parts of an old mincer, and some perforated sheet zinc left over from the pantry window. (Sheet zinc is easily cut with old scissors.) It is stuck directly on to hardboard and painted with enamels. The background was painted last. Use transparent glue.

NEWSPAPER CHURCH *(page 116)*

Newsprint of varying typeface can be used with effect to create a feeling of texture as illustrated in this design of a church. By using plain coloured paper for the sky and principal parts of the building, newsprint of different sizes can be used at different angles to complete the overall impression. Initially, draw the design out very carefully on cardboard and use a PVA adhesive or paper glue.

FELT HOUSE *(page 117, bottom left)*

Use natural or brick coloured felt, cut into mosaic patterns. Draw the building carefully on to the board and fill in one section at a time. You will see from the photograph how the felt has been cut into these small shapes to simulate the effect of brickwork and stone.

LIONS *(right)*

This design must be carefully drawn out before cutting felt. When the pattern is drawn to your liking, cover the board with a plain colour background, and using a rubber-based adhesive, start glueing down the shapes, superimposing tree and leaf shapes over each other, and spots and patterns over the lions.

Keep the centre of the design uncluttered, as the animals should be the focal point in this composition. Fine lines can be added either by cutting narrow strips of felt, or with wool or cord.

THATCHED COTTAGE *(page 117, top)*

This picture illustrates the way nature's own materials may be used in the art of collage.

Natural straws and dried flowers have been used here against a painted sky. Twigs, ferns, etc., are suitable for this type of design.

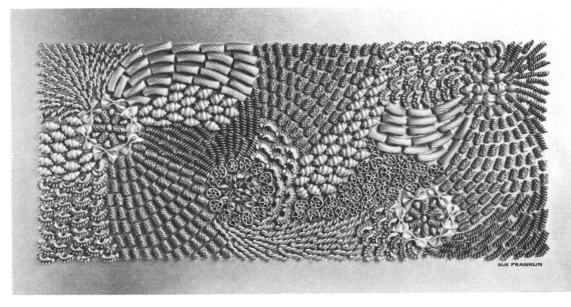

String and Raffia Figures

We shall never know who started making figures from rope. Perhaps the first one ever was made in some moment of imaginative playfulness. But, whatever its origins, there is no doubt that for many years young and old have derived great enjoyment from making all kinds of figures from rope, these have usually been reinforced with wire. One doesn't need to be an artist to do it, and the materials you need are cheap and easily obtainable. The results of your efforts may be given away as small but attractive gifts or they may be kept as eye-catching decorations on a book-shelf or on top of a writing-desk. We have collected rope figures from a number of people in the hope of inspiring similar efforts from others who may either lack confidence or be temporarily short of new ideas. Beginners should start with simple figures before going on to the more advanced projects which they will then be able to tackle without difficulty. When you have acquired a certain familiarity with the material and the general method, we hope that you will develop your own ideas and create new and original figures.

CAMEL

The reason for portraying the gift-bearing camel on page 122 is not because it is simple to make but because it is so attractive. Beginners are advised to attempt some of the figures on the following pages, however, before coming back to the camel.

The camel is made from hemp rope. The legs are made from two pieces, each 50cm (19½in) long, and a piece 70cm (27⅗in) long makes up the body from head to tail. The tail is plaited from thin twine. After drawing the wire through the rope (see below for directions) the ends are bound with natural raffia. The two 50cm pieces are tied to the body in three places as shown in the photograph. An end of the third piece is bent and covered completely with natural raffia for the head, behind which the mane hanging over the neck is made from frayed-out rope fibres. Two eyes are added to the head. Then the rest of the 70cm length is bent into two humps and tied to the legs. Finally, the camel is given a pair of reins made out of red raffia, after which the small packages may be hung about the humps as shown. This is, of course, a very pleasant way of presenting small trinkets as gifts.

Rope-figures are usually made from sisal-rope reinforced down the middle with wire. You can buy the rope already reinforced or you may decide to add the wire yourself. The wire is easier to insert if you bend over about 1cm (⅖in) at the end to avoid a sharp point of wire catching in the rope.

Because sisal-rope frays so easily, the ends that we cut must be immediately bound with raffia. In addition to rope, wire and raffia we shall need an all-purpose glue, a pair of scissors, a darning needle and pliers.

The basic structure of the figures is the same, with one piece of rope for the main torso from head to tail and two pieces for the legs. The measurements that we have suggested for some of the figures are merely to help those who are doing this for the first time. Naturally, you may choose to make them either bigger or smaller.

THE CAT

The cat on page 121, bottom left measures 21cm (8⅖in) from ears to tail, and the legs are made from two pieces each measuring 12cm (4⅘in). The ends of the leg-pieces are bound with raffia as shown. The head-binding leaves a piece free, which is then coated with adhesive, forked and cut into two ears which fit as shown. The tail is likewise stiffened with adhesive and then cut into a point. Finally, all three pieces are bound together in the middle.

THE LITTLE HORSE

The mane of the little horse (left) is made from loops of raffia drawn under the strands of the rope. One end of the rope is frayed out into a bushy tail. From ears to tail, one piece of rope is 30cm (11⅘in) long, while the legs consist of two pieces each 16cm (6⅖in) long.

THE IBEX

From the same size of rope we can make the ibex shown on page 121, top, in the same

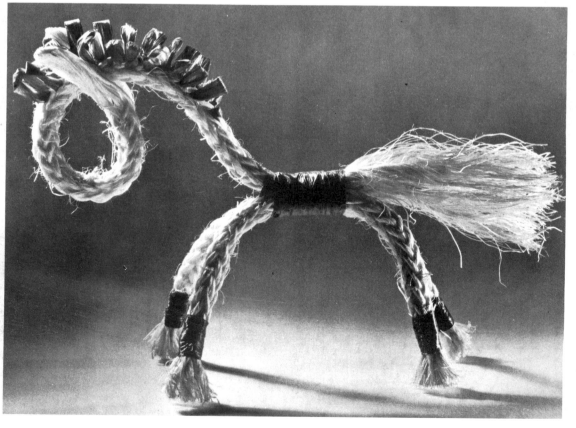

or the mouth and throat. The back consists of large loops of the pulled-out sisal-fibres, and the legs consist of a separate piece bent into shape and sewn to the body as shown.

DOLLS

The jolly little dolls on pages 124, 126, top and 127 (top and bottom right), were made from wire (for the skeleton), wooden balls (for the head) and raffia (for the body and costume). Since rope is dispensed with, you will need a lot more raffia than usual.

A one metre (39$\frac{1}{3}$in) length of wire is bent in half and pushed through the wooden ball so that it emerges at the other end and the loop will take the rich raffia wig in any variety of styles and hold it in place by drawing it back a little into the ball once the raffia has been pushed through it. Next, direct from the head, bend the arms into shape, following with the legs, bending the wire back on itself at each hand and foot, and finally fixing the ends of the wire into the head. The arms and legs are again bent so

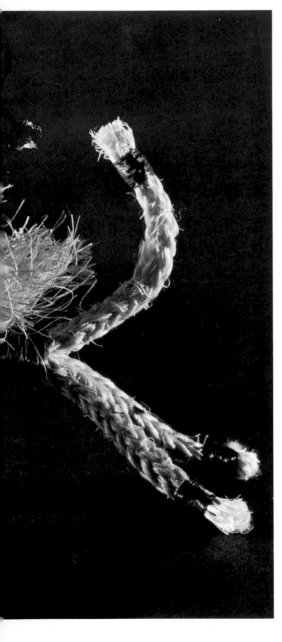

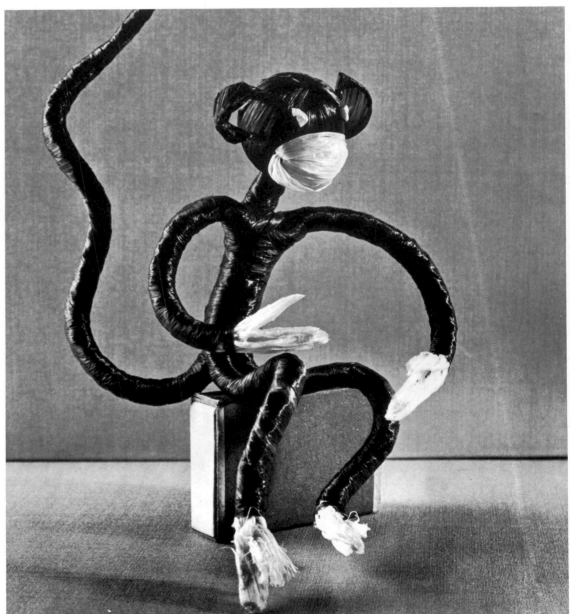

that the figure takes up the particular posture you have in mind for your doll. Further refinements are a matter of taste and imagination. Raffia is available in a variety of attractive colours which can be combined in a number of ways to produce a range of striking figures.

THE BLACK POODLE

The black poodle below is made from electric wire. We leave a piece standing for the tail and wind the rest about forty times around a thick knitting-needle. We slide the spiral off the needle and wind it in four complete coils with loose ends. Thus we have the first leg. The loose wire is now drawn upwards through the leg and coiled into a spiral for the second leg. Having done this and drawn up the wire through the leg in the same way, the next step is to complete the hind-quarters. The length of the body is double-coiled firmly from the back to the front where a small loop is left to draw through the wire before starting on the fore-legs. The neck and snout are next, the latter coiled about five times. The wire is run through the spiral and the ears are bent into shape. The poodle has a double-crown on the head, made from a spiral of about 20—25 loops and bent into shape. Finally, the neck spiral is coiled, the wire is drawn through one of the fore-legs and cut. The poodle is ready for a walk!

THE CHINAMAN AND THE LADY

The Chinaman (page 125) and the lady on page 127, bottom left are a couple of very attractive figures made from sisal rope, standing 17cm (7in) high, with a raffia-covered cotton ball for a head in each case. The Chinaman has close-fitting black trousers and an attractive blue smock made from broad strands of smoothed-out raffia. The puff-sleeves are tied at the wrist. The hat, and the stands supporting each figure, are woven from raffia.

The lady on page 127 has an elaborate black coiffure, decorated with two glass-top pins, a long red and yellow dress of raffia, a blue sash tied in a large bow at the back, and a small blue bow on each wrist. In her left hand, she carries a genuine Chinese parasol.

Both figures are a delightful project for anyone who is painstaking and patient as well as appreciative of form and colour.

DOLLS

On pages 125 and 126, bottom left, you will find the kind of doll that costs next to nothing to make as you will only use the odds and ends that are already available around you.

The body is made from sisal-rope in the usual way while the head is again a cotton-ball covered with stockinette. The shaggy-haired doll illustrated on page 125, top left, has a wooden ball for a head. In each case,

e magnificent heads of hair are made from
ightly-coloured scraps of sheep's wool.
heir outfits consist of coloured slacks and
nics, and carefully stitched tiny leather
oes.

THER HORSES

beautiful variation of the little horse shown
 page 120 is illustrated on page 122. For
e big horse you will need 75cm (29½in)
 middle-thickness cord—for the body, head
d tail, 35cm (13¾in); for the legs, two
0cm (7⅞in) lengths. The head is 5½cm
⅛in) long, the ears approximately 3cm
⅕in).
 When winding the raffia, begin with a
oss between the ears so as to make sure it
esn't slide) after that wind the raffia
ound the head, first rather coarsely to-
ards the mouth, then back again towards
e ears with raffia. For the mane insert 4cm
⅝in) strands of sisal fibre by means of a
ochet-needle and use a comb to get it to
ok neat. Now make the tail by simply
ravelling the sisal-cord; fix the body and
g-pieces together with raffia; finally partly
over the legs with raffia and glue on two
all pieces of leather to simulate eyes.
 The small horse is made from 50cm
9½in) of cord thinner than that used for the
g one. You will need a 22cm (8½in) length
 the head, body and tail and two 14cm
½in) pieces for the legs. The head is
proximately 4cm (1½in) long, the ears
cm (⅝in).

Acknowledgements

CANDLE MAKING
Text by Anne Collings, David Constable and Randal Marr. Model candles by Anne Collings, David Constable, Randal Marr, Roderick Mee, Mina Rashide, Des Parker, Bob Spackman and Simon Hole. Photographs by Robert Harding and drawings by Colin Elgie. Ceramic candle holders by Jean Hull. Showroom backgrounds by Amos Reynolds Ltd. of Sutton. Original English ©, Search Press Limited, London.

BATIK
Original material by Tony Bachem-Heinen, prepared for this book by Christian Albrecht. Workings by Tony Bachem-Heinen, Rose Zimmermann, Elisabeth Schaaf and Siglinde Kauls. Photographs and drawings by Paul Bachem. Original German © Christophorus Verlag Herder GmbM, Freiburg im Breisgau, West Germany.

WORKING WITH METAL FOILS
Original material by Agnes Gaensslen, prepared for this book by Raymond German. Models by the author, Hans Gaensslen and Karl Maier. Drawings by Agnes Gaensslen. Photographs by Toni Schneiders. Original German © Christophorus Verlag Herder GmbM, Freiburg im Breisgau, West Germany.

SOFT TOYS
Edited by Hilary Turnbull of Atlas Handicrafts. Embroidered Ball by Sheila Graham, Tipo Buffo by Zoe Martin, Cuddly Cub by B. C. Whiley, Ming-Soo, the Japanese puppet, by Ingrid Rowling and Puff, the Baby Dragon by Patricia Capon. Photographs by Robert Harding. All the models were entries in the Woman's Realm Leisure Crafts Competition, run in co-operation with the National Federation of Women's Institutes. Original English ©, Search Press Limited, London.

BASKET WEAVING
Original Material by Werner Klipfel, prepared for this book by Rodelinde Albrecht. Working by Edeltrud Barth, Klaus-Peter Busch, Wolfgang Engler, Ursula Horst, Margarete Hüglin, Rosemarie Keller, Rosemarie Klipfel, Ulrike Nutz, Hildegard Schneidemesser, Irmgard Stührk and Gertrud Trotter. Photographs by Toni Schneiders and Alfred Kutschera. Drawings by Werner Roll. Original German © Christophorus Verlag Herder GmbM, Freiburg im Breisgau, West Germany.

WORKING WITH LEATHER
Original material by Gerhard Frank, prepared for this book by Rodelinde Albrecht. Workings by Stefanie Beckman, Gerlinde Beiter, Ingeburg Böhringer, Sr. M. Isentrud Brokamp, Regina Buchner, Helga Dorer, Gerd Frank, Renate Frank and Inge Schmitz. Photographs by Toni Schneiders and Alfred Kutschera. Drawings by Alfred Kutschera. Original German © Christophorus Verlag Herder GmbM, Freiburg im Breisgau, West Germany.

MOBILES
Original material edited by Marta Högemann and Erich Priester, prepared for this book by Verena Smith. Workings by Ursula Binder, Doris Buchholz, Adelheid Degen and Trudi Högemann. Photographs by Toni Schneiders and Alfred Kutschera. Drawings by Willy Kretzer. Original German © Christophorus Verlag Herder GmbM, Freiburg im Breisgau, West Germany.

DECORATIONS FROM DRIED FLOWERS AND GRASSES
Original material by Hans Fasold, prepared for this book by Raymon German. Workings by the author, Hildegard Boje, Gertrud Fasold Ludwina Korselt, Anusch Krmadjian, Heimschule Reitenbuch Wladimir Schukow. Arthur Schulz and Hans Thiel. Photographs b Toni Schneiders. Drawings by Willi Harwerth. Original German © Christophorus Verlag Herder GmbM, Freiburg im Breisgau, Wes Germany.

PUPPETS
Original material by Erich Priester, prepared for this book by Christia Albrecht. Models by Hans Quast, Rosemarie Zimmermann and th students of the Katholisches Kindergärtnerinnen- Seminar, Freibur Photographs by Toni Schneiders and World-Press-Photo. Drawing by Peter Jürgen Wilhelm. Original German © Christophorus Verla Herder GmbM, Freiburg im Breisgau, West Germany.

HOMEMADE ENAMEL JEWELRY
Original material by Rose Zimmermann, prepared for this book b Verena Smith. Additional designs by Edzard Seeger. Photographs b Toni Schneiders. Drawings by Willy Kretzer. Original German © Christophorus Verlag Herder GmbM, Freiburg im Breisgau, Wes Germany.

THINGS TO MAKE FROM ODDS AND ENDS
Text and drawings by Elisabeth Anzlinger, photographs by To Schneiders. Original German © Christophorus Verlag Herder GmbM Freiburg im Breisgau, West Germany.

CLAY MODELLING
Original material by Gerhard Frank, prepared for this book b Raymond German. Workings by the author and students of th Padagogischen Hochschule, Freiburg. Photographs by To Schneiders and Alfred Kutschera. Drawings by Willy Kretzer. Origin German © Christophorus Verlag Herder GmbM, Freiburg im Breisga West Germany.

PAPER, SCISSORS AND PASTE
Original material by Margrit Winkelmann, prepared for this book b Verena Smith. Texts by Margrit Winkelmann and Peter Jäcke Photographs by Toni Schneiders and Alfred Kutschera. Original Ge man © Christophorus Verlag Herder GmbM, Freiburg im Breisga West Germany.

COLLAGE
Text and some collages by Beryle Bell. Remaining collages b entrants in the Woman's Realm Leisure Crafts Competition. Phote graphs by Robert Harding. Original English © Search Press Limite London.

STRING AND RAFFIA FIGURES
Original material by Marta Högemann and Erich Priester, prepare for this book by Raymond German. Workings by Ingeborg Springe Sigrid Dreher, Gretel Klinger, Doris Bucholtz, Ursula Bindner, an Maria Wolski. Photographs by Toni Schneiders. Drawings by Wil Kretzer. Original German © Christophorus Verlag Herder GmbM Freiburg im Breisgau, West Germany.